I0560288

You Believe Me?

A True Story of Thriving after 30 Years
of Parental Brainwashing & Abuse

Tambryn Crimson-Dahn

Infinite Impressions Publishing

For more information, email Inquiries@iip-books.com

ISBN: 979-8-9908008-8-5

To my wonderful husband and sons, who gave me the motivation to keep working at becoming all that I can be.

To my amazing parents for helping me out of the broken home when no one else would believe me.

To my beyond stellar two besties for always being there and also for being my rocks when the seas get rough.

To my former therapists. Thank you Cathy for putting up with me and providing me with the tools I needed to become healthy. Thank you Julie for all your continued support, both personally and professionally, which helped me, and my company, to thrive.

To all the people who are enduring or have endured abuse, depression, addiction, or trauma. I hope you find peace along your journey toward a better life, and rise above all challenges with fierce strength and dedication. I dedicate this book to you, as well as the fallen warriors: Alicia, Joe, Carolyn, Solomon, Marlena "Missy" Golding, Steven M. Francek, and Amanda Bassett. Rest in peace, courageous warriors. I hope publishing my story creates more awareness and prevents others from such fate, as I almost was as well.

Contents

An Opening Reflection

I t was never my intention to make the memories within these pages public. This narrative was originally written at the advice of my therapist at the time as a way to help me process the trauma. Although I had once believed my story to be unique to me, the more I shared while working with others with trauma, depression, and anxiety, the more I felt called to share my story publicly. In a nutshell, I was raised by two undiagnosed, mentally ill parents. My mother was beyond codependent, as she was obsessed with every person she had a relationship with, and chose selective amnesia as her coping technique in regards to the abuse she and I endured. My father was an extreme narcissist who was covertly abusive and expertly manipulative, as his claims coupled with his feigned empathy were very convincing. It wasn't until several years later, during my psychology schooling, that I realized that he possessed all the symptoms of a rare mental illness called FDIA (Factitious Disorder Imposed on Another), formerly called Munchausen by Proxy.

After years of divulging my story to those I had worked with in the restaurant industry, I realized that many people had experienced some form of psychological abuse and manipulation, albeit not to the extent that I experienced it. Later on, I went on to pursue a career in fitness, then even later, pivoted and ultimately ended up working in mental health. With every person I encountered and subsequently helped, people kept urging me to share my story, telling me how much it inspired them and gave them hope when they were about to give up. After six years of refusing to do so, I now realize, thanks to my clients, that the time has come to share everything that I experienced.

Sharing this story is not something I want to do. I am a very private person and sharing this will no doubt draw attention to my inconspicuous self. I value my anonymity, but realize that, after this book is officially published, I may no longer have that anymore. However, I have a strong desire to help others and that desire cannot be ignored or quieted. When I was at my worst, about to end it all, the one thing that stopped me was hearing the severely traumatic story of a friend of mine and finding inspiration in the fact that she still had the courage to keep fighting, even when things were beyond tough. I took an oath as a mental health practitioner and as a human being, to ensure that I would do everything within my power to prevent others from feeling as helpless, alone, and worthless as my so-called support system had once allowed me to. In publishing this story, it is my hope that others will realize that when all seems lost and they feel completely alone, there is someone else who has suffered. There is someone else who has been nearly invisible. There is someone else who has also initially given up after the world gave up on them. There is someone else who has hated themselves and made bad decisions resulting from trauma. And, on the flip side, there is someone else who has made a complete turnaround mentally, physically, emotionally, financially, personally, and professionally. There is someone else who turned night into day, trauma into triumph, dark into light, miraculously turned their curse into a gift.

I share this story boldly in the hopes that others who are hurting can see that there is hope even when all seems lost, that there is strength in your story, that you are not a failure. It certainly won't be easy but you are worth the effort.

This book is for all the other kids who think that even God doesn't want them and for all the people who feel stuck in bad situations. If publishing this journal helps just one hopeless kid, one person about to give up, one person who feels stuck, one person being abused, then it'll all be worth the exposure I really don't want. If this book helps just one person, it will make sacrificing my anonymity worthwhile.

Thank you for buying this book and for reading my crazy story. Some of the funds earned from your purchase will aid my colleagues and I toward helping others who need it. Much appreciation to you, whoever you may be.

Above all, never forget this: you are enough, even if no one else is telling you so. And know that even if no one else does, I believe in you.

Trigger Warning

This book is a memoir, recounting the author's memories. Many of the events herein were occurring simultaneously, and there are over thirty years of memories and emotions transcribed into one simplified narrative. Names have been changed to protect the privacy of those described within these memories. Certain events have been condensed and some dialogue has been recreated. My intent is not to cause any harm resulting from the publishing of my story. Any perceived offense to any individual or organization is entirely unintentional.

While the following narrative was published with the intention of helping others, it contains several various accounts of traumatic events described in a very graphic manner. For some individuals, especially those who have endured similar situations, this could trigger certain unpleasant and negative memories and emotions. This book is suitable for adults only.

Humor Warning

The humor used within this narrative may not be for everyone. Humor has been a big help in my coping with the trauma that I have endured. The humor within the following pages is meant to help negate the heaviness of the situations and dark emotions to make my story an easier read rather than recounting one negative event after another. One might say that humor lightens the load, so to speak, of the intensity of the trauma described herein. I am a big believer of the phrase, "I'd rather laugh than cry," meaning that I choose to laugh at the pain I have lived through rather than cry about it. Crying tends to carry sadness, whereas laughing makes one feel better. It is my hope that my readers find the humor used within the following pages to be a delightful break from the heavy trauma, instead of finding it offensive or insensitive.

Where it All Began

The Journal Entries

After many years of remembering every traumatic memory and realizing that things were not my fault, I was doing much better. I was working full time and had even gone to school. Still, I realized that I was not yet one hundred percent and I was experiencing a lot of rumination. I kept mentally reliving the trauma of the fact that no one had been willing to ask me my side of things and that was mainly why Mother was so truly ill. When I shared this with my former therapist — who had since become a friend — I realized I hadn't truly processed the painful truth: my mother, with whom I once had an intense attachment, had become so ill that she inadvertently chose to stay with her abuser. She couldn't see that, because he refuses to change, I can never be healthy as long as he remains in my life. She refuses to see that he hurts her, and refuses to acknowledge any of the problems that he had caused me, resulting in several extreme, long lasting hurts, habits, and hangups that would go on to negatively affect my life. I had known that she was sick but I still hadn't processed the fact that she really truly was as ill as she is. Although I had processed the events from the memories I had recovered, I still had yet to process the loss of my once beloved mother. This was different from losing a loved one who dies. I knew that Mother was physically alive, yet mentally dead, so to speak, incapable of remembering the hurt and the pain, too scared, weak and fragile to even be willing to acknowledge the ugly, horrific truth of our lives.

Because of these things, my counselor friend suggested that I journal about my thoughts and feelings, and that doing so would help me to really acknowledge and comprehend them, while also serving to help me overcome the facts of my painful reality. These are those entries and this is my story.

Monday, May 23, 2022:

How do I even begin to process the hurt that the mother that raised me caused? I know she wasn't trying to hurt me, and that she didn't mean to become so ill, but I watched it all happen, slowly, over time, from a young age. I warned everyone about the truths that were happening behind closed doors but no one believed me. I know it didn't seem plausible with all the medication I was on, the fact that I had severe depression and severe anxiety that caused constant panic attacks and pain to which I could barely function, and especially since they adopted me into that hell. I wasn't able to hold down a job, afraid to leave the house, and afraid to socialize. But not because of the reasons that he had convinced everyone of. In reality, the truth was buried beneath a deep, dark tunnel of unending, sadistic lies.

Her constant excuses for him were disgusting. They deeply hurt me and kept me, and herself, sick. "He didn't mean it," she would constantly tell me. So he continues to insult and berate me and it's ok because that's just who he is? Hell no! It wasn't ok and it still isn't ok. It will never be ok for any individual to mistreat another person, especially someone who was supposedly his daughter. I always heard the dreaded, "He didn't mean it. He has had a hard life. His daddy walked out on him when he was just a little boy. He had switches taken to him in the back yard!" And that makes his rude, cruel actions ok? Alright, if she's gonna keep score: My daddy never loved me or ever wanted me, evident from him telling me "We had a lot more fun before you came along, then we couldn't have any fun anymore." My daddy controlled me and ruled my life, instilling fear in me. My daddy told me what to think, who to be, what I should wear, what I should listen to, and who I should hang out with. My daddy was so polite to everyone he knew, yet behind closed doors, behind the sadistic shroud, I always heard about how these people were "insecure", "idiots", "can't prioritize", "not very pretty", "such a dip", "real winners", "should be shot". My daddy talked to me about my mother behind her back about how "mommy's a pussy" and how she should "shut up, bitch." My daddy is the reason I can't be a police officer like I wanted to, because apparently, he's the reason I can't hear well. I never asked them to adopt me, especially not now that I realize that in HIS mind, I was their slave, obligated to do their every bidding. And when I didn't, I was given the name, "God Damn it, Eliza!" I only heard that 20 times a day until I believed I was a god-damned human being with absolutely no value.

My mom used to be my hero. When I was a kid, the house was always clean and organized. She was the nicest person, she used to defend me from the only time she witnessed him raise a hand to me. And now, she believes she can't do anything right. She cannot stand to look at herself in the mirror because she doesn't like who's staring back at her. She's a complete hoarder. She's always under the weather. She refuses to see that he isn't a good person. She has no memory of any of the traumatic events she or I have endured. Any time I would recount the trauma, which I did too many times to even try to count, she would say, "I don't remember that." I would always respond with, "That's the problem, Mom." He would convince her that the trauma never happened, and she would forget, never to remember again, no matter how many times I reminded her. Yet he would remember it to use against me at his next convenience.

What happened to the mom I had when I was a kid? What happened to her confidence? What happened to her organization? What happened to her playfulness? What happened to my supporter? What happened to my protector? What happened to my hero? Why wouldn't anyone I told the truth to believe me? Is it completely impossible that he has a fake personality that he displays to everyone in public, yet is a completely different person behind closed doors? It's completely impossible that the only time that he revealed his true self was behind the shroud he showed only to his immediate family? Everyone who knew him would shower me with compliments and tell me what a kind person I was. They would give me job references and speak highly of me to anyone who asked about me. But when I hinted at the truth saying, "Behind closed doors, things are going on that shouldn't be," they acted like I was the worst person in the world and accused me of making that up. People never questioned him and always believed his lies without hesitation. Some people would respond by ghosting me, never to be heard from again. Several others would change the subject and then later say to me, "Your parents are sooo nice, and I totally understand older people." A few others who claimed to be so close to myself and the family would accuse me of exaggerating.

I wasn't able to function, I get it, but why was it so completely impossible to them that it was because of things going on behind closed doors that he would never allow anyone else to witness? Their inability to believe me led to my mothers eventual demise. My perfect mom, my hero, my idol, is now the 2.0 version of the most repulsive, repugnant person that I have ever had the displeasure of meeting. And I had to live with that person! I used to say to her, "I can't stand him! He's repulsive and repugnant to me in every way, shape, and form!" And she would defend him, "E-liz-a! That is your daddy and he loves you! He does a lot for you! Don't you ever talk about him like that!" She couldn't realize what was plain as day to me even as a child. And neither could any of the other adults around?!

I grew up believing that I wasn't enough. My thought dialogue was: If I was enough for mom, she wouldn't need him. If I was enough for mom, then she'd realize the truth. If I was a good daughter, my mother would realize she is being abused. If I was a good daughter, my mom would have the strength to leave him so we can both be healthy. If I could just get up off the couch like everyone else, I would be able to hold down a job and get us both out of here. If I was a good enough human, I wouldn't need all the medications. If I could "human" correctly, I would be able to breathe in my own house. Everyone else could, and even though I, the therapist, the psychiatrist, and the pulmonologist said that they should have the house checked for mold, my parents knew what was best for me, so obviously it really was in my head. I guessed that I *was* autistic. If I wasn't, everyone wouldn't be treating me like I was. My poor parents had to take care of my piece-of-shit, worthless, waste of space self, because they were obligated to. Since they can't afford to do anything fun or go on trips anywhere because of me, I'd made plans to kill myself with all my pills once my scripts got refilled. That way, I was sure to succeed and save them from the burden of having me in their lives. I believed that I was everyone's favorite burden. Nice to me only because they were trying to make me feel better. They weren't cold enough to tell me the truth of how horrible I actually was.

Fuck them and fuck that. Fuck him for making her and me so sick. Fuck him for choosing a life of hurt and wrongdoing, intentionally doing things to hurt both of us. Fuck her for not seeing the truth, even when I told her over and over and over, for years and years and years. Fuck everyone who knows them for refusing to believe me. Fuck them for never asking me about my side of things instead of just assuming his perceived goodness. Fuck them for always believing him hook, line, and sinker. Emphasis on sinker, because he had sunk my life and is continuing to sink hers. Fuck him for continuing to bad mouth me and continuing to hurt her. Fuck her for choosing to be, and stay, so sick. Fuck the old me for believing his lies for so long, for continuing to try to make her see the light and wasting so many years on her that I will never get back. Fuck all of them for still continuing to believe his lies that he is no doubt telling about me in order to preserve his perceived image of goodness.

I don't understand how someone can be so unempathetic. I really don't. Aren't hurts supposed to make one *more* empathetic? Even after all that, I still have no idea how to even begin processing all the trauma and hurt and confusion he caused. And he caused it intentionally. What do I even do with that? How do I even begin to process all of that? I have so many memories that I can't even begin to know what to do with, even years after I've gotten out of that broken home. But one thing I know for sure is, I will never forget any of them. I will have them for the rest of my life, whether I like it or not.

And thus the reason for rumination...

Tuesday, May 24, 2022:

I need to process the things that happened to me, but...what does that even mean... to fully process something? I know in order to do that, I have to relive the traumatic events that I endured, but I keep doing that in my head on a daily basis. Maybe if I take the time to write all of this out, I will be able to process all of the things that happened. I agree with my counselor friend. I'm somehow hung up on the fact that my mother is too far gone. I haven't fully processed that and all the events that transpired behind closed doors. That the last text communication I had with her was the final straw that caused such a strong trigger with my PTSD while I was working in the restaurant industry. I have since deleted the text, but I can still see the very words and spacing and the gray text bubble that those words were encased in.

Monday, May 30, 2022:

Mom...a word that at one point in life held so much meaning to me. Such a simple word, only one syllable. So simple that it can be said at a very young age. It can also be learned at a young age, including the implied meaning of the word.

As a child, the word meant unconditional love and adoration. It meant protector and hero. It meant organizer and house keeper. It meant personal chef and also personal nurse. But looking back now, it also meant peace-keeper and negotiator. It meant warden's guard and spy. It meant that as long as both she and I complied, life would be good. And if we didn't...well I would discover the results of that years later.

Tuesday, May 31, 2022:

I have figured out how to abolish the self-loathing. But now, with this journaling, I find that I still very much resent and have anger towards everyone who knows them. These people were all given 31 years to believe me but instead chose not to even listen to my side of it. Because of all of them, I didn't get the help I needed when I should've gotten it, which caused me to still have problems even though I've been out of that broken home for years. Most hurtful of all, their choice to not even admit that there could be more to the story other than what he claimed, which led to my mother's continued sickness. She never got the help she needed, and now it's too late. She's been with her abuser for 52 years. At this point in time she is no longer capable of ever healing. She can never become the person she once was. The loving, helpful, heroic mother I once had has now become my abuser's 2.0. I know I have said this before, but I still can't process it. Maybe if I keep saying it over and over again, it will help. Have the words not sunk into my brain? I think it was the shock of it all. I spent years praying to God to bring her out of the darkness of his abuse and into the light of her reality, which was also my reality. I had spent years begging her to get me out of there, every night screaming at her the exact same plea, all to no avail. Her final text to me still haunts me. I still see the words so clearly in my mind, punctuation, emojis, and all.

I think what hurts me the most is knowing that when I had to leave her behind, she never realized that she had a choice, and must feel like I don't want her. That couldn't be farther from the truth. I became healthy enough to realize the truth: he hadn't just been abusing me, he had been abusing both of us all along. I had also become healthy enough to realize that neither one of us would ever be able to function in society or even as healthy human beings unless we removed ourselves from the situation. The day I realized she was afraid to leave, I decided that I would stay too. I couldn't just leave her there to be abused alone so I tried to make her see that that was what would happen once I left. I told her every night for years that I would take any and every opportunity to get out of there and would never look back. I also told her every night for two years that, if I ever got out of that environment, if he was still in the picture, I wouldn't be. I told her how much it hurt me to watch him insult and berate her. I told her how much it hurt me to hear him saying so many bad things about her to me when she wasn't around. Then she would inevitably ask, "What is he saying?" I would always reply, "I can't tell you because I don't have the heart to make you cry and hurt you like he does."

Like I said before, maybe I need to type all these truths here and now, onto this laptop. Maybe doing that will unearth the reality that I find it so difficult to grasp; maybe it will unearth not just in print, but also in my heart, mind, and soul.

Well, here it goes…

My mother is no longer and can no longer be who she once was.

My mother is full-on Stockholm Syndrome and will never be able to realize his lies aren't the truth.

My father has damaged my mother to the extent that she believes she is worthless and can't do anything right.

My mother believes that she is inadequate and inferior in every way.

My mother thinks she doesn't deserve any praise that is given to her.

My beautiful mother feels ugly because of his insults and does not like to see herself in the mirror.

My mother was so convinced that his lies were the truth that she was afraid to even try to get me into a safe environment.

My mother cannot tell up from down or black from white.

My mother cannot think, feel, or believe on her own, she only knows what he tells her.

My mother is physically alive, but emotionally and mentally my father's 2.0.

My mother believes his lie that I am ungrateful for everything she did for me.

My mother believes his lie that I am a horrible daughter and person.

My mother believes that I have forsaken and abandoned her.

My mother believes that I do not love her, and that she is not worth loving.

My mother believes that her being out of my life is what I want and doesn't understand that I had no choice but to leave in order to keep myself healthy.

My mother believes that she failed me and that she is a horrible mother, which my father is no doubt continuing to tell her.

My mother can't believe that I chose to distance myself from him and is not capable of realizing that he is a really bad person, and is the one I am distancing myself from, and that I can no longer stand to watch him abuse and berate her.

My mother is feeling fractured and broken and doesn't even realize how aware of it I am, and how much it hurts that I cannot do anything about it since she refuses to see it or leave her abuser.

My mother accused me of breaking her heart when I broke things off finally, not even realizing that she broke mine over 20 years prior.

My mother believes that the reason for God not answering her prayers is because she doesn't deserve to have them answered.

My mother feels like God has forsaken her.

My mother believes that even God doesn't want her.

My mother believes that her husband keeps her around and "puts up with her" because he is obligated, and therefore is such an awesome person for putting up with her instead of leaving her.

My mother feels like she has no value.

I know all of these thoughts and feelings she has because I once had all of those same thoughts and feelings. Now that I have gotten out of that hell of a home, I realize that all those things were never true.

I said a lot of prayers growing up. I prayed that God would remove the agonizing pain I felt every day that paralyzed me from functioning normally. Before I got healthy, I had believed that God had forsaken me. I had believed that even He didn't want me. Now that I am healthy, I realize that in order for me to be able to heal, I needed to remove myself from the stimuli that was causing the agony and atrophy. But more importantly, I prayed that He would open my mother's eyes to the abuse we were enduring. I told Him that it was too late for me, I was inadequate and inferior in every way, but told Him that He should save her, because unlike me, she didn't deserve to live that way. She deserved much better. I even told her that many, many times, all to no avail.

So again, maybe I should repeat it over and over again to make myself process it.

My father ruined my mother.

My father hurt my mother.

My father damaged my mother.

My father insulted my mother daily.

My father berated my mother daily.

My father never loved my mother.

My father manipulated my mother for his own personal gain.

My father abused my mother.

My father brainwashed my mother.

My father turned everyone in my former life against me and now they all believe that I am the one at fault, and that he's done nothing wrong.

My father killed who I used to be, but, unlike my mother, I was reborn.

My father killed my mother and she can't come back.

My father killed my mother and she can't come back.

My father killed my mother and she can't come back!

My father killed my mother and she can't come back!

MY FATHER KILLED MY MOTHER AND SHE CAN'T COME BACK!!!

MY FATHER KILLED MY MOTHER AND SHE CAN'T COME BACK!!!!!

NO MATTER HOW MUCH I WANT HER BACK SHE CAN'T COME BACK BECAUSE HE KILLED HER AND SHE'S GONE!

And there's nothing else I can do other than that.

I think that's the real problem. I still love her. I never wanted this for any of us but here we are. It happened, and now she's too far gone. All because everyone wanted to believe the pretty lie instead of the ugly truth. So instead they left me all alone to deal with the truth and to deal with all of the destructive behaviors caused by this traumatic truth.

Nice, huh?

Yeah, I've had a pretty heavy life. Guess it makes complete sense that I'm a weightlifter and bodybuilder now. Lifting heavy shit until it's not heavy anymore, either emotionally or physically, is what I've done my whole life. Maybe that's why I'm so short. I got weighed down so much that I never grew.

The Recollections

Age 0

The very first traumatic memory that I can recall happened at the very young age of several months old, although I don't know exactly how many. According to my mother, this happened in a local public swimming club.

I remember suddenly, out of nowhere, my eyes opened wide as could be and I was upside down, fully immersed in the water of the pool. I know other people were in the pool, too, as I could see pairs of legs, although I wasn't focused on them very much. I was too concerned about my seemingly impending death. I was too young to even speak yet, so I am not sure how I knew that my body was not equipped to exist under water for long periods of time. "Well," I said to myself in my head, "this is it. It's been a great life." I entered a somewhat mindless state, as if I were in some sort of trance. It was then that vague and unclear thoughts about being near death flooded my mind. Then I thought to myself, "This is it, I'm gonna die." I floated there in the water, completely unable to help my infant self. I wasn't feeling scared at all. Instead, I felt a sense of acceptance and peace about the whole situation. I felt certain that I would die very soon. Although I was too young to have been taught anything about God and Heaven, I felt acceptance and felt extremely calm. I sensed that I would be in a better place after I died, and that, in that place, everything would be completely fine, and I would never worry again.

Then, after what seemed like two minutes, I saw Mother's arms reaching into the water to grab me, and I knew I was about to be rescued. I have no recollection of what happened next. I don't even remember coming out from under the water.

When disclosing these thoughts to my therapist years later, Mother had no idea that I even remembered any of these things, completely surprised that I did. According to her, I had been in an inflatable froggy-shaped floatation device in the pool. It had a rope attached to it that she had been using to pull me around with her in the pool. She claimed that I hadn't been under the water long at all and when she pulled me out of the pool, I hadn't reacted much at all and was unfazed by the situation.

It's weird that Mother stated that I didn't have much of a reaction, yet I clearly recall the trauma, fear, and uncertainty from that event. I now wonder if maybe I actually was really scared when she pulled me out and that Father convinced her otherwise. Maybe that was another time she was brainwashed. I guess at this point no one will ever really know.

Age 2:

As I sit here typing this, I am surrounded by many of the things that Mother had hand crafted for me. One of the projects we made together was a set of styrofoam skulls. We each decorated one. It hurts knowing that she cared enough to spend quality time together on several occasions yet now cannot be in my life because it causes me to be extremely unhealthy. I know it was too painful for her to handle the truth about our living situation, but that left me to handle that agonizing truth all alone, starting from a very young and impressionable age.

The first memory I have of being scared and feeling unsafe was when I was only two years of age. It must have been nighttime because it was dark outside, evident by the fact that I was in the guest room with the lights off. Why I was there, I have absolutely no idea. I recall nothing about what happened before I went in there. Maybe I had intentionally tried to isolate myself from my father? All that I remember is being inside the guest room with Father and hearing him mutter under his breath "dumb ass".

Even though I was only two, I knew that those words were directed at me. I was instantly very hurt and scared. Something deep within me knew something wasn't right. I had no idea what I had done wrong to deserve being called those mean words, and had no idea how I should react. The one thing I did know was that I wanted my mommy.

Father left the room, and I was left alone, now sobbing, feeling isolated and scared with no one to comfort me.

I'm not sure how much time passed, or if it was much time at all, but it became evident that he noticed I hadn't followed him downstairs. He walked back into the room and I became startled. I hadn't expected him to come back.

He asked me grumpily, "What're you crying about?"

Sensing his unreceptiveness from his previous derogatory comment, I was afraid to tell the truth. Even at that age, I somehow realized that the truth would be unpleasant to him.

For fear of upsetting him, I replied, "Nothing." I was too young to know what else to say.

Knowing that Mother would protect me, I asked, "Where's mom?"

He responded shortly with, "She's not home." Then he left the room again.

After what seemed like an eternity, Mother finally returned home. I could hear her conversing with Father as they approached the guest room, with him telling her something to the gist of, "She's been crying and won't tell me why."

Mother entered the guest room and knelt beside me, wiping the tears from my face as she embraced me. What a warm, tender, and loving embrace it was. Much different from how our embraces would end up feeling years later.

"What's wrong?" she questioned.

Father was still standing in the doorway, so I leaned toward mother's ear and whispered, "He called me a dumb-ass!"

The scowl of anger and outrage was displayed instantly on my defender's face. She shot up and quickly turned toward him, screaming, "You called her a *what*?!!!"

He acted like he had no idea what I was talking about and asked her what I had said.

When she told him, he yelled, "*What?!*" with a definite increase in octave.

Quickly, he claimed to her that he had said "Jesus," and that I had misheard.

Without much thought, she looked at me and told me that he hadn't really called me what I had thought I had heard.

It became my assumption that I had been mistaken and therefore had no reason to be upset. Then I apologized to my father, and my mother.

Obviously, Mother is my protector and wouldn't believe my father if that really was what he said. Afterall, she's my mom, it's her job to protect me, and her job to know if something wrong happened. If it had, her motherly senses would be able to sniff out any wrongdoers and any perpetrators would surely have been persecuted. Besides, at that age, I was too young to really know what was going on in the world, so I obviously had my own perception of things.

Looking back now, I realize she agreed much too fast to her husband's answer. I see now that there must have been other times in which she immediately believed the quick answers he always seemed to have. As kids, we don't notice the things that appear as red flags like we do once we grow into adulthood. Often, we are unintentionally made to believe that our thoughts and feelings aren't as accurate as those of an adult. All of these factors — including my mother being manipulated into believing certain things, and my father ensuring that only I witnessed them — ultimately led to the disbelief, disregard, and ridicule I would face throughout my painful life.

Age 3

In the middle of one of my late night toddler fits, Father came into my room since it was his turn to care for me. I don't remember why I was crying, but Father seemed inconvenienced by it, evident by the deep creases forming a scowl on his face.

"Stop your crying!" he quickly demanded.

"I want Mom!" I screamed back, completely unbothered by his grumpiness and harshness.

"Stop crying!" he demanded again.

But my young toddler self, desiring Mom's comfortable, warm demeanor, pressed on, "I want Mom!"

Completely fed up with my tantrum, he picked me up and bent me over his leg.

This took me by complete surprise and I found his actions rather rash.

What is the big deal? I'm just a young kid who wants my Mommy.

When I looked up at him and saw his hand towering high above my rear end, I realized his intent was to spank me.

Fearing the impending pain, I began screaming frantically, feeling terrified and confused as to why my crying was apparently a big crime. I strained my tiny voice, shouting as loud as I could at the top of my lungs, desperately hoping Mother would hear my plea, "I want Mom! I want Mom!"

Just then, Mother casually opened the door, while simultaneously tying her robe. As soon as she looked up and took notice of the scene before her, her eyes widened in horror, dropping her robe ties and screaming at the top of her lungs, "Paul! What're you doing?!"

Father immediately set me down as she rushed towards me.

She embraced me tightly as she consoled me. Then she told him never to raise a hand to me again.

He left the hallway and walked back to their room, obviously disgruntled as he muttered something barely audible under his breath, but seemingly happy that the loudness I had been causing had stopped.

Mother remained out in the hall with me until I calmed down, then proceeded to take me back to bed.

At that moment, she became my hero. At that very moment, I learned that she would always protect me and do what was best for me. I respected her for understanding how afraid I had been and felt thankful to have a mom who protected me from it.

I arrived at the conclusion that that must be why there was a mom and a dad. The dad was the provider for the family and protected them from the big problems of the world, like crime and other scary things on the news. The mom's job was to nurture the kids and work a little less, and to keep the father's temper in check.

When it came down to it, I felt that they loved me and took good care of me.

Who was I to be upset at Father for having a temper? After all, they accepted me even though I sometimes woke them up in the middle of the night.

Obviously, I had mixed signals and conflicting feelings from a young age. Raise your hand if you can relate.

Age 4

Mother had been raised Catholic since her childhood, and was still extremely religious. She prayed before bed every night, but never attended church like most religious people. One of her most prized possessions was her mother's Bible, which she displayed on a side table in the living room. I never saw her read it, though, or any other Bible for that matter. She was however an open and honest God-fearing woman, she was always overly concerned with doing the right thing, and could never do anything wrong.

Father, on the other hand, seemed much more laid back about life in general. He was never concerned with what anyone else thought or how they felt about things, meaning if someone had a problem with him or the way he did things, he didn't care. Contrary to Mother, he never prayed and did not show much concern about whether something was right or wrong. He even once looked at me sternly and said, "Don't ever read the Bible. Everything in it is crap."

Mother had given me a few books about God, which she had read aloud to me from a young age. She taught me about God and how He was always watching us, "so we should never do anything to disobey our parents or do anything that would hurt other people."

"So God is like Santa Claus?" I questioned Mother.

"In a way," she responded.

I didn't understand the need for the universe to have two Santa Claus like figures with two different names.

And why is God so much better than Santa Claus? He doesn't give me presents every year.

Even at such an immature age, I was able to understand on some level the vast difference between Mother and Father's religious beliefs, and found it sort of odd on some level. Yet I didn't know enough to question anything.

Later that same year, I said a prayer asking God to give me the ability to know ahead of time about things that would happen in the future. My reasoning behind this request was so that I would know when Father was about to be angry. I figured that if I could somehow know beforehand when he was about to get upset, then I would be able to run and hide before the fireworks started. That way, I would always be able to avoid him instead of being hit.

It never occurred to me until years later that maybe I didn't deserve such treatment, or that I had a choice in fighting back...or that it was okay to.

Age 5

As I was sitting at the kitchen table playing with a coloring book, Mother was preparing lunch and Father was passing in and out of the kitchen as he completed household chores.

Mother noticed that I was staring off into the distance, so she asked me, "What are you thinking about, Eliza?"

I paused, then replied, "I just suddenly have this feeling from deep inside me."

"What do you mean?" Mother asked, concerned that I might not be feeling well. "What kind of feeling?"

Again I paused, searching for the words that would correctly describe the strange, intuitive feeling I was experiencing. "Like I was created to accomplish something really great and out of the ordinary."

As Father walked by and heard this, he joined Mother in chuckling aloud, viewing my words as nothing more than a silly childhood whim.

Years later I would learn that this was no whim, but a glimpse at my destiny.

Late one night, Mother was sitting on the couch, demanding that I go brush my teeth "this instant!", as I had been refusing.

In true toddler fashion, I continued to put up a fuss with no regard for what either of my parents thought or how annoyed they felt.

They each continued insisting, attempting several more pleas, yet I kept refusing.

A few minutes later, my childlike tantrum escalated to launching the toothpaste tube at Mother, hitting her in the face.

I immediately knew I had done wrong, watching her face display shock and pain as she screamed, "Ouch!"

Father became so enraged that he whisked me off, not at all gently, to the bathroom, where he proceeded to yell at me.

"God damn it, Eliza! What did you do that for?! You should've brushed your teeth like we asked you to and we wouldn't have this problem!"

He left the room to go check in on his wife, who was still crying with shock.

He came back quickly, however, telling me that the toothpaste tube had hit her in the eye with the pointy edge of the tube, and that it had sliced her eyeball, and as a result "she might even lose her eye."

Instantly overcome with guilt and shame, and believing what a horrible child I must be, I sobbed loudly enough to shake the house, so to speak. I was too upset to say or think anything, all I could manage to do was feel extremely guilty, believing that I was the lowest of the low.

After several long minutes passed, Mother entered the bathroom where I was still sobbing profusely. She questioned why I was still crying.

Obviously still overcome with guilt, shame, and now, self-hatred at what I had done, I couldn't help but continue to bawl.

Eventually, she told me to stop.

But that didn't stop my despair.

Before she could ask me again, I shouted beneath my sobs, "I'm sorry! I'm so sorry! I didn't mean it!"

My bawling continued, and I added, "I didn't mean to take your eye!"

"What are you talking about?" she asked, confused.

I hadn't even looked up, until now. I saw that not only was her eye intact, there was also no presence of blood.

I suddenly stopped crying and stared at her, puzzled.

"Why did you think I would lose my eye?" she questioned.

I responded with, "Dad told me the tube cut your eyeball and you might lose it."

She turned to her husband with an angry glare that would've ended his life if looks could kill.

"Paul!" she exclaimed.

After that, she said nothing else to him for the rest of the night.

Although I thought it was an extreme thing for a father to do, my young mind rationalized that it really must not be, otherwise my caring, loving, protecting mother would never have allowed him to get away with it unscathed.

Although the incident lasted a mere several minutes of my lifetime, it left a scar of an imprint on my brain for the rest of the night, only to become repressed until many long years later.

Upon finally remembering, I brought it up to Mother, who responded with the ever-present, "I don't remember that."

She never acted as if she disbelieved any of the memories I would later bring to her attention, yet she never seemed to find any of them of any significance.

PSA: If you're a crier, make sure you have tissues before reading any further. (Like you need me to tell you that this is going to be a bumpy ride after what you just read.)

Age 6

At the age of 6, I was diagnosed with allergies and asthma, which Mother reacted to by crying profusely. She was so worried about me that she would forbid me to do any activities that could expose me to any allergens. I was not permitted to play at anyone's house who had pets, or to play outside if the pollen count was too high, or if someone was burning leaves, or if someone had cut their grass. And I was forbidden to play in the woods with the neighborhood kids, which caused other kids to refer to me as a "buzz kill", therefore I was often left out of neighborhood games.

Because of Mother's extreme paranoia, my body never had the opportunity to build a defense against those allergens, which affected me quite frequently the older I got.

Having no siblings to share the pain or abuse with was bad enough. Even worse, because of my allergies, I also had no cuddly companions when and where I needed them most, after being slapped and/or berated by Father. The aquatic frogs I had as pets didn't adequately meet my comfort or companion needs.

That same year, Mother was ironically unfazed by the discovery that I had a profound hearing loss, the cause of which I would later find out from my ENT could have only been caused by domestic abuse. Mother had mentioned that I used to hold loud baby toys up to my bad ear, so the event most likely occurred during infancy. To this day, I still don't remember anything like that, which I guess makes sense considering that I would've been so young.

One day, there was a repairman at the house for reasons currently un- remembered, but what I do remember is the man having to shut off the water temporarily.

I had just used the bathroom and then realized that I wouldn't be able to wash my hands because of the lack of water. Too nervous about germs to simply wait until later to wash my hands (an unrecognized symptom of my germaphobia that would later develop) I became upset to the point that I sought Father out to complain that I "needed" to wash my hands.

He told me to just go without washing them for now, but when I kept persisting about my need for sanitary hands, he grew extremely put out.

I recall strikingly clearly being outside the bathroom in the downstairs hallway.

Wishing to end my, as I'm sure he phrased it, "bitching," Father start- ed screaming at me. While his exact words escape me, the fear in my then-young mind hasn't. I remember backing away from him, walking slowly backward all the way down to the end of the hallway, near the base of the stairs. Heavily annoyed, he followed me as I went.

Suddenly, it was as if something in him snapped. In the blink of an eye, he had grabbed tightly onto each of my arms, and shoved me against the wall with a jerk, which hit my back and head with a thud.

My eyes widened, and I suddenly sensed that I might be hanging. Upon looking down, I saw my feet dangling in midair, as I had been lifted about 5 inches off the floor. My heart raced in my chest as he just held me there, glaring at me intently, eyes reflecting his anger at and hatred of me.

Terrified, there was nothing I could do. I was entrapped in his strong and enraged grip.

While I don't remember what happened after that, I'll say this much: I have a very memorable precursor towards my journey of becoming a germaphobe.

At the small school I attended, instead of a library, we had a van that would come to the school parking lot. It was exciting for us kids, as it was like a temporary escape for us, making some of us feel like we had snuck off of school grounds, even temporarily.

During one visit, I was about to return the library book that I had previously checked out.

"Oh," my classmate said, pointing to one of the books, "I want that one next!"

"Okay," I replied as I handed her the book. I was so happy that I was able to give her the book before someone else got it.

Later that week, Mother asked me if I had returned that particular library book, saying that she had been notified that I hadn't returned it.

"I returned it," I said.

"Then why did they say that they don't have it?" questioned Mother. "Did they ask Aria?"

Mother replied, "Why would they ask her?"

"Because I gave it to her since she wanted it," I stated.

"Honey," Mother said, "You are supposed to give it to the librarian so she can scan it first. Otherwise they don't know where their books are."

"Oh," I sensed that I had done something wrong. "I'm sorry."

"It's okay," Mother replied. "I'll be at your school at the same time as the library van this week, so I'll straighten it out with them then."

Later on, Mother explained to the librarian what had happened. "So I'm sorry about that, but she *did* return the book, so we shouldn't be paying the late fee."

"I can't waive the fee," stated the librarian strictly.

Mother's jaw dropped, then she asked, "Why not? I told you what happened."

"It's not our fault that your daughter didn't follow procedure." responded the librarian.

"But she didn't know," Mother said in a pleading tone.

"It's policy ma'am," replied the librarian. "We can't break policy for one person."

"But she's just a kid!" Mother grew incredulous. "Did you teach Eliza how to check out books?"

"It's not our responsibility to teach them that, ma'am." said the librarian. "I'm sorry."

With that comment, Mother was speechless.

Suddenly, I felt guilty, as if I had gotten my mother in trouble.

This is all my fault. Mother wouldn't have gotten scolded by the mean librarian if I had done things right. Now Father will be so mad at me, and at Mother too. And it's all my fault.

Age 7

For fire safety day, my school had the local fire department bring out a model home on wheels to demonstrate to all the children what to do and how to react in the event of a fire. The team of firemen led by example of how to remain calm, ways to help breathing within a field of smoke, and how to exit safely out a bedroom window. After the demonstration, each child was led through this obstacle course of safety, which made me nervous, as the end of this safety course was out the top window of this truck that resembled a house. I had a fear of heights, so having to climb out a high window and onto a ladder was quite terrifying to my seven year old self.

When my turn arrived, I made my way out of the smoky room, up the stairs, and through the hallway into the bedroom, where I was then instructed to climb out the window. Terrified, but realizing I had no choice in the matter, I swung my leg out the window, and onto the ladder. As I attempted to continue downward, I realized that my pants were stuck to part of the ladder. Realizing I could not move, I grew terrified as I realized I was stuck at this height, forced to endure my fear of heights.

Fear flooded my entire body as I squirmed while yelling frantically, "I'm stuck! I'm stuck!"

Oblivious to my deep fear, one of my classmates pointed at me and then said, "Eliza's stuck!"

Then he and all of my other classmates began laughing hysterically.

The firemen helped me off of the ladder, and to this day I still have no idea what part of my clothing caused me to become stuck.

After they helped me down, the firemen demanded order from the audience, one of them saying, "Fire safety is no laughing matter. In any real instance of fire, what you would do is immediately go over and help Eliza to get down and away from the fire for her safety."

Those comments only embarrassed me more, and a sense of shame and inferiority shadowed over me.

What a day! Forced to deal with my fear of heights and also made a mockery of all at once. And that was all before lunch. I wonder what other chaos I could've gotten into given more embarrassment. Hmm, maybe situations like this are how sitcoms are born.

One day, some neighbors called the house and asked Father if he would help them move a piece of heavy furniture after they hauled it to their house in a few more days. Of course, Father agreed with a smile, then hung up the phone.

"Well shit," he said.

"What?" asked Mother.

"I have to help Gerald move a piece of heavy furniture," he replied.

Later when Mother left the room, Father told me, "Don't tell Mom, but I really don't want to help move the furniture, but I can't say no. I'm obligated."

"What's obligated?" I asked.

"It's something you have to do, even if you don't want to," he explained. "If I don't help them, I'll look bad."

Reflecting on this instance, I now realize why I had believed that I was obligated to keep an abusive family in my life. This was the first of many instances where Father would ingrain in me, "Ya can't say no" in reference to either something that someone wanted him to do or something that he wanted me to do.

Having a neighbor my age who was just as manipulative and abusive as my father didn't do me any favors.

This neighbor was about a year older than I, and lived right next door. Her younger brother was just as bad. Once he, completely out of the blue, grabbed a bunch of my hairs with his fist, and slowly pulled them out of my head, literally bringing tears to my eyes.

When I told Mother what he had done, she paused, then responded simply with, "*Ow!*"

So...you're not going to defend me?

On another occasion, my parents and I had gone over to their house for dinner. After we ate, the adults were talking and we kids were playing behind the couch. I accidentally leaned on my knees, which were both still covered with huge scabs from having fallen off my bike earlier in the week.

I thought to myself out loud, "Oh, I better not let my knees get scratched."

The neighbor girl, Junie, replied, "Why not?"

"Because if they get scratched, they will bleed." I replied, wondering how she didn't already know this.

Without hesitation, Junie's face quickly changed into a malice-ridden scowl as she pretended to claw at my scabs.

This intentionally harmful act blew my mind. I grew extremely uneasy and scared, feeling as if anyone who would gain pleasure from someone else's pain was downright evil and would probably become a murderer later in life.

I attempted to fight her off, swatting her arms away from me as I fumbled around trying to find a way to get up from the floor so I could get away.

Luckily, her father heard all this commotion, and he asked us what we were doing.

Seizing the opportunity for help, I announced that Junie was trying to scratch my scabs. Her father said sternly to her, "Don't do that, Junie!"

I peered into my parents' eyes with a helpless, puppy dog-like plea on my face, hoping that they would understand my extreme discomfort at the circumstances and take it upon themselves to remove me from the premises. My expectations, however, were met with much disappointment, as they looked away from me like nothing unusual had even happened and went about the rest of their night.

I was then convinced that I had a demon living next door to me, and the worst part was that my parents didn't even seem to see or acknowledge it.

Later on, that same family was invited to our house for one of Mother's home cooked dinners.

Mother intentionally left the front door open, the screen door allowing the perfectly temperature summer air to enter our house.

It had already grown dark outside, so my father didn't notice when the neighbors arrived in the midst of his private discussion.

He said, "That Junie's such a little dip."

Mother noticed that the family had arrived and were standing on the other side of the screen door. She used her stereotypical scolding comment of, "*Paul!*"

Completely oblivious to the fact that they were there, Father responded, "*What?*"

"They're right there!" Mother pointed out, embarrassment showing clearly on her face.

He looked over and froze momentarily, realizing he had been caught. Not knowing what else to do, he suddenly smiled widely and emitted a happy sounding, forced, "He-ey!" as if nothing had even happened.

I didn't realize until many years later that that was the way my father acted in front of everyone outside of the home: fake.

On another occasion, Junie and I had been making invitations for a party we decided we were going to have. It was another one of the many things we planned and never followed through on at that young, eager age.

She suddenly said, "Let's play blink the eye."

Never having heard of such a game, I asked, "What's that?"

She said casually, "I take this pen and point it at your eye, and you blink before it pokes you."

Suddenly I became very uncomfortable, and a weird feeling that I would later come to know as anxiety flooded my whole body. Even at that young age, something deep within me knew that this just didn't seem right, or even normal. But neither one of my parents had ever remotely given any hints to Junie's strange behavior, so I had come to believe that this was just normal.

I had never known how to say no (a trait that I later discovered was ingrained in me by my mother's habits) so I attempted a distraction instead.

"Hang on, let me finish this invitation," I proclaimed.

My young, naïve brain assumed that if I kept the piece of paper in front of my face, it would prevent Junie from going ahead with the game. Within seconds, however, I learned the hard way that I was very mistaken.

Suddenly I felt a stabbing pain—literally—in my left eyeball, and I had no idea what was going on. Instinctively, I let out the biggest scream I could, louder than I ever had before. I removed the paper from my face to see what had caused it, and saw Junie staring at me in shock, so I knew instantly that there was a problem. I screamed at the top of my lungs, nothing but hatred and, secretly, fear in my voice. My yelling was shrill and high pitched, almost resembling a high octane falsetto type of sound as I screamed at her, "Junie! I'll never play with you again!"

Selfishly fearing for herself, Junie bolted up and fled the scene, running out the door as if she were being hunted.

This left me all by myself, feeling assaulted, insignificant, and abandoned.

Within seconds, Father came in from mowing the lawn, and after that all I remember is waking up on the couch in the living room with a cold compress over my injured eye.

After several more minutes, Junie and her father were standing over me, as her father had brought her to apologize. Junie offered her forced attempt at reconciling, looking down at the floor the whole time. Realizing even at that age that she had been forced to apologize, I truly felt that she didn't really mean it. Whether she actually was sorry or not I will never really know.

Her father continued telling Junie how horrible her actions were and making a point of saying how lucky she was that her cruel actions didn't poke my eye out and send me to the hospital.

What do you mean she's lucky?! Aren't I the lucky one, having to put up with your crazy daughter?

Too young and also, at the time, too traumatized to really understand the situation back then, I now understand what a bullet I dodged, or I guess I should say pen.

Even though I obviously still have my eye, I later discovered that I have a scratch on my retina. While there's no way to know what it's from, there's always the possibility that it was caused by her cruel actions.

When later recounting that story to a recovery group, I was asked by one of the members of the group why I was allowed to play with Junie. Realizing finally what a great question that was, I then proceeded to ask Mother.

Her response was, "Well everyone always got together as neighbors back then and I didn't feel comfortable causing a tiff."

Wow, I must really not be worth defending.

That proves the old saying wrong. The pen isn't always mightier than the sword. Thank goodness, otherwise I would only have one eye now.

Age 8

One night after dinner, I was eating Tootsie Rolls for dessert. Troubled by the bits of paper still stuck on the candy, I complained to Father that I couldn't eat my dessert because some of the paper was stuck.

"It's okay to eat it that way." He responded.

"It's okay to eat some paper?" I asked inquisitively, suddenly curious about the workings of the human body, which could obviously somehow digest tiny paper pieces.

"Sure," he responded. "Eating paper's good for you."

Even at eight years old, this seemed an odd response to me. I had previously learned about fiber and its role in aiding digestion, yet this seemed strange. Even then I could tell that it seemed that Father didn't want to be bothered with providing an explanation.

Suspecting that he was offering me a quick answer to shut me up, I thought up a plan to get him to admit that his words were unreasonable.

Drawing his eyes in my direction so that he would see me in action, I said, "Look! It's easier now." I then proceeded to place another Tootsie Roll in my mouth, wrapper and all.

Father's eyes widened as he exclaimed, "Don't do that!"

After pulling the candy out of my mouth, I asked, "Why?"

"It's not good to eat the whole piece of paper," he admitted.

That was the first time I realized that Father would say anything to make things more convenient for himself.

I would later learn that these techniques had an actual term: manipulation.

Convinced by Father's manipulative prodding, I joined the third grade basketball team. I wasn't very good, especially since I'm short and never really cared for the game.

One night, the school district had all the teams from every school meet at one of the schools for a dinner, during which a photographer and news reporter were present.

Before the event, my father had become quite excited, telling me that I would probably get my picture in the paper, asking me, "Wouldn't that be cool?"

I nodded, although at that age, I honestly only cared because I was afraid of disappointing him, thus making him mad.

It really didn't matter to me. I knew my only friend wouldn't find it interesting, and neither would my classmates, as the only ones who cared about the newspaper at all were the adults.

When it came time for the event, my parents and I traveled to a school that was foreign to me to eat dinner with a bunch of people who were also foreign to me, other than my teammates of course. We all ate dinner in the cafeteria, at a bunch of large round tables, then after dinner, the pictures were taken of each team.

Father leaned in and ordered me, "Go over to that lady with the camera and tell her that your dad said if she doesn't put *your* picture in the paper, he'll beat her butt."

Having heard many derogatory things about everyone behind closed doors quite regularly, I didn't find this to be a strange or unsettling request, so of course I did it.

The woman seemed quite taken aback at my words, yet quickly gathered herself, following my gaze in Father's direction.

He offered her a cocky yet threatening wave along with his smirk of a smile.

The woman then asked me, "What's your name?"

Still completely unaware that this was highly unusual, not to mention inappropriate, I told her, "Eliza Stater."

She then jotted it down in her notebook.

Days later, I heard my father exclaim from the other room, "God damn it!"

From his tone of voice, it sounded like something was wrong, I guessed maybe a car had stopped running or something semi-pivotal of that nature.

"What?" asked Mother.

"That dumb ass deliberately didn't put Eliza's picture in the paper!" he responded angrily. "God damn it!"

Because of the frequency of derogatory comments as well as controlling behavior from Father, I spent my childhood believing that this was totally normal. I assumed that all fathers acted similarly behind closed doors. I thought that a man showed his true colors to immediate family only, and put on a façade in front of everyone else. At that young age, I mistook that for closeness, believing that since men supposedly weren't supposed to show emotion, that was how the wife and children knew he was close to them.

It wasn't until I was seventeen years of age that I started to realize how inappropriate Father's behavior was and that it was far from normal.

Age 9

One day while my parents went out alone together, they left me in the care of a family friend, who also had kids.

Their friend told her youngest son and I that she was going to have a business meeting soon, and that when her coworker arrived, we were to be "very quiet" for her "important meeting."

Their meeting commenced quickly after her coworker's arrival, during which time her son, all of five years old, took it upon himself to discover the difference between male and female anatomy.

As I was lying on the couch, he crawled up beside me and did not hesitate to blatantly shove his hand down my pants and into my underwear.

Obviously uncomfortable, I called into the other room to his mother, shouting, "Tammy, help!"

When she entered the room, I was horrified to find that she was completely oblivious to the fear on my face. She spoke sternly with authority, ordering, "Nope. Quiet. Play quietly until the meeting is over."

She didn't say it rudely or derogatorily yet she was completely lacking the empathy I so desperately needed in that crucial moment in my young, impressionable life.

I felt that I had no choice other than to just lay there and continue being molested, which lasted the duration of the meeting, seemingly for hours, although it probably wasn't really.

After the meeting concluded, the mother came back into the room, thanking us both for being "so good" during the meeting, still completely clueless that I had just been violated, and then furthermore made unallowed to have a voice. I left their house that day feeling exposed, raw, and uncomfortable. This was one of many times where I felt as if I was never heard and that I may as well be invisible.

I was too afraid to say anything to Mother. That woman was her friend, so how could I tarnish her opinion of her and her son? Afterall, I knew everyone would assume I was "just a kid," as Father had so often pointed out to people. Neither of my parents cared about anything or did anything about the traumatic events in the past that had made me uncomfortable, so why would this be any different?

That isn't what I thought they meant when I heard from that boy's school that he "plays well with others."

Age 10

In fourth grade, my teacher noticed that I was shy and socially awkward, and that I had a big vocabulary, which are traits of a form of autism, called Asperger's. She contacted my parents informing them, recommending that they have me tested. The autism screening came back negative, but they diagnosed me with ADD and prescribed medication.

No one ever asked me where I had learned so many advanced words, but if they had, I would've told them that my father taught them to me.

Honestly, I wasn't eager to learn all the words he wanted me to know, but I had figured out that anytime I didn't, he would then refer to me as a "dumb ass."

Therefore, why wouldn't I learn those big words? Why wouldn't his constant belittling not deprive me of any confidence? I was so afraid to socialize due to the belief that no one would like me. After all, if my own father didn't like me, why would anyone else?

On another occasion that same year, I was in a classroom with a bunch of students. I randomly looked around the room, and then a teacher I didn't know, Miss Frawley, met my gaze, smiling at me from across the room.

I reacted by looking away shyly, yet something about this woman really stuck with me. I quickly became obsessed with this woman, wanting to know more about her. I would watch her every move and intentionally try to be in the lunch line when I knew she would pass through the cafeteria. I wrote her letters telling her how much I admired her, which in hindsight, must have made her uncomfortable that I had fixated on her to that extent. I used to tell everyone in school that she was my older sister, and I was so proud anytime anyone believed me. My obsession escalated to the point that I thought about Miss Frawley the majority of the time, and even asked Miss Frawley if I could live with her. I didn't realize at the time that my behavior was strange

At this time, my mother would always go out of her way to get together with people, or even just to talk to them on the phone when they called, always claiming that it wasn't a bad time, even when it really was.

Later, I would come to realize that she is extremely codependent, which in hindsight partially explained my fixation with Miss Frawley.

Years later, I came to realize that I saw genuine kindness and empathy in that first smile from Miss Frawley. These were things that I wasn't seeing at home. On some level, I knew that my parents weren't taking care of me the way parents are supposed to. I realize now that, subconsciously, I felt that Miss Frawley wouldn't treat me badly or allow me harm, which was more than I could say for my parents.

This fixation caused an even further separation between my father and I at that adolescent age. He told me that I was "not right in the head." I understand now that my actions were far from healthy, yet his insulting way of trying to tell my young self that only made me hate him and distrust him further.

Really? Mother allows him to abuse me and I'm not right in the head? Of course not, Mother's obsession with him is convenient for him, whereas my obsession with Miss Frawley made him look bad.

Age 11

That was the year of Father's fiftieth birthday, a birthday many people would soon forget. A group of three female students from Father's class at the school where he taught phoned the house several days before, gaining Mother's permission to have a huge yard sign put up for the occasion.

It read, "Happy 50th Birthday! From the Bananarama gang." Father later revealed this to be the nickname that he had given the group of these particular girls.

When his birthday arrived, he noticed the sign outside the house when he went to get the newspaper.

Although I had still been asleep that morning, I later learned that Father had become angry when he had seen the sign. He wasn't happy that his age had been advertised publicly to everyone on the street. I imagine most people would share his sentiment.

Mother seemed clueless as to that fact, stating that she had thought it was sweet of the girls, who "probably didn't even realize it would embarrass you." Some of the neighbors even shared Mother's sentiment, saying how nice they thought it was that Father's students admired him enough to put up a yard sign to celebrate him.

Father told Mother, "You really shouldn't have let them do that without asking me."

Mother took note of the disappointment on Father's face on her behalf, and responded with a shy, "I'm sorry. I was only trying to help. I thought I was doing the right thing."

Perhaps this event played a pivotal role in shaping Mother's future inability to ever do anything without Father's input.

I asked my mother if I could go next door to neighbor Cathy Robbins' house, and of course she okayed it. There were two Cathy's in our neighborhood. I made sure I clarified which one.

After having been at the Robbins' house for several hours and since it was a beautiful day, her younger sister and I went to sit outside on their front porch swing.

Neither one of us noticed when my mother pulled up at the house...that is, until she started screaming at me at the top of her lungs.

"Eliza! Get over here right this instant!" Her voice sounded more erratic than I had ever heard it.

It was odd to me that she sounded mad. I ran over to see what I had done wrong, although I knew I hadn't done anything.

When I approached her, still in her car with her window rolled down, it was evident by her red, watery face that she had been crying.

"Where have you been?" Not leaving me any room for a word in edgewise, she continued, "I have been worried sick! I called over to the Willis' house and when they said you weren't there, I started driving around looking for you! Do you know that I started flagging people down and asking if they'd seen you? Neighbor Bill even started driving around looking for you, too!"

I paused, confused as to why she was so mad, and waiting for her to realize her error, given that she had found me at the Robbins' house, where the other Cathy lived.

After several moments longer, I realized she was too flooded with anger to realize her error, so I said, "I told you Cathy Robbins."

She paused, finally realizing her error.

"Oh, okay." she offered timidly, seemingly embarrassed as she looked away from me and proceeded to drive into the garage hurriedly.

If she was so concerned, why was her reaction to yell at me? Why was she acting like I disobeyed her? Didn't she know me better than that? And if she was so concerned, why wasn't her first reaction to get out of the car and hold me tightly in her arms, instead of yelling at me like I was a horrible person?

She later seemed embarrassed when neighbors called up to ask if I had been located, acting nonchalantly as if she hadn't been immensely worried, saying that it had been "just one of those things that happens with children when they tell you the wrong name." I now recognize these as yet more red flags of my childhood.

One night, I was asked to stay the night at a classmate's house from school. It wasn't my first time spending the night at this friend's house, so I knew that I was guaranteed to have fun, as I always had before. Her younger sister had also invited a friend to stay over, so it was a fun little foursome. We stayed up late into the night, long after her parents had gone to bed. My classmate's sister decided she wanted to play doctor, and proceeded to pretend to examine her friend. The younger sister then made her way towards her friend's genital area, which made her clearly uncomfortable. She voiced this awkward feeling by saying, "You're done with me. It's someone else's turn now." Of course the little girl wouldn't turn to her sister, so that only left me to "examine."

"No," I resisted as I pushed her away, a feeling of extreme uneasiness growing steadily in the pit of my stomach.

She persisted, however, and I had the thought that my friends probably would sense my uneasiness and tell her to stop.

No one said anything, however, and instead chose to watch as the little girl felt up my private area.

I was extremely uncomfortable, but must have subconsciously realized that I had been through a similar situation years prior, so I shut down, overcome with fear and shame. I was ashamed that I had no say in who touched my body. Ashamed that I had no control over what others did to me. And ashamed that I was not strong enough to push people away.

Subconsciously, I believed that I wasn't worthy of anyone defending me, and felt like I was on display as everyone simply watched me be violated, once again. I would go on to stay at this same classmate's house a few more times within the next few years, always excited to do so, as it would take me many more years before this memory would resurface.

That was the year I started isolating myself from people. I was afraid to admit to anyone that I was feeling...different. I wasn't sure why, but I felt down most of the time those days, like life was dull and not really worth living. This is when feelings of suicidal ideation first developed in me. I didn't necessarily want to die, but I knew with every fiber of my being that I wasn't even living. I kept these feelings to myself, as I assumed these were very uncommon emotions, and that something was seriously wrong with me. Quite frankly, I was terrified, because I secretly thought I was seriously messed up in the head.

Age 12

My home life was less than desirable, yet what I hated the most was school. I was usually not noticeable at all, but for some reason, I had caught the attention of a group of boys on the back of the bus.

They had annoyed me to begin with, being loud and boisterous, whereas I was the quiet type that was always alone with few friends. And they were always "cool" at least having each other to "hang out with" whereas I had only one friend.

One day, they were louder and more annoying than usual, thanks to a bag of candy that one of them had smuggled into their bookbag. Now sharing this candy thus quite hyped up on sugar, they decided to start spitting candy across the aisle of the bus. After several minutes they had grown bored of that.

"Hey," one of them said. "Watch this."

He proceeded to spit candy straight ahead instead of into the aisles, and it landed, of all places, in my hair. Lucky me!

Instantly, I was enraged, with several choice insults running through my mind, yet I was too shy, awkward, and scared to even acknowledge that I was completely aware of this. Instead, I hoped that it would stop, and even prayed that it would. Yet this was one of many instances where my prayers and attempts at chanting mentally, hoping for some kind of magic mind-control, would be met with much disappointment, as it continued.

The group of boys continued to laugh hysterically as each candy projectile stuck to my hair.

When I got off the bus and into the house, Mother noticed the candy pieces in my hair, and asked me why I had candy in my hair. Too embarrassed to admit that I had been bullied, or that I was aware that I had candy in my hair, I acted like I hadn't known that the pieces were in my hair. I had secretly been hoping that, since it was pretty obvious what had happened, she would console me and hold me while I cried. Yet again, my hopes were unanswered and I was greatly disappointed as I walked to my room, filled with shame and self-hatred. I hated myself for not being able to stand up for myself. And I hated Mother for never standing up for herself or me, and for never being able to teach me how to.

That was the first time in my life I had to pick candy out of my hair. It would happen again in the hallways of my high school with students laughing hysterically as they "hit the dorky redhead target."

There was also another time in high school when some boys got into a shoving match and I happened to be in the way. One of the boys who got shoved was thrown into me and I was subsequently knocked down while holding textbooks in my arms. Having no defense with arms that were occupied, I rolled onto my back like a turtle, and the entire hallway laughed at me.

And then there was the time a mean girl insulted me, and boys who launched spit balls at me, and a teacher who ignored me, and another girl who tried to avoid eating lunch with me...

Oh, sorry, I got off on a tangent about being bullied at school. But that's not what this narrative is supposed to be about, so I digress.

Where was I? Oh yeah.

I had the neighbor kids over one night for my twelfth birthday party, listening to music in the basement with the strobe lights, as was our custom.

I went upstairs to go to the bathroom, then ended up getting into some kind of an altercation with Father along the way back downstairs.

I still don't remember any of the details, other than coming back down the basement stairs silently, with tears in my eyes and with my right hand on my right cheek. My neighbors were all chatting, then one of them, Michelle, saw me, her eyes rising with concern instantly. My other neighbors all followed her gaze to look at me, all equally concerned.

"What's wrong?" Michelle asked.

Still in shock, I paused before finally replying in a daze, "He hit me! He hit me!"

"What?!" exclaimed my neighbor Sally.

"Who hit you?" Michelle questioned.

"My Dad." I stammered at last. "My Dad hit me!"

Their reactions of shock indicated to me that maybe, just maybe, what was going on in my house actually wasn't normal...or right.

I thought that soon everyone in the area might find out what he had done, because the neighbor kids would all surely go tell their parents once they got back home.

For the next several days, my body was filled with butterflies. I braced myself mentally for phone calls to the house with potential inquiries, and a huge potential downfall between my father and I during which I might be hurt. I was so afraid, but as it turns out, I had nothing to worry about, because nothing ever happened.

I began wondering why.

Did everyone's parents not believe me? Did they think I was making it up, or exaggerating? Or had my father convinced them of such? Or was it a messy situation that everyone else decided they didn't want to get involved in? Or were people afraid, like my mother had been years ago, of causing a riff if it turned out to be my imagination? Or maybe it was just my imagination?

No one ever acted like anything could even be wrong, and I was always told by friends and neighbors how nice my parents were.

Yeah, that's it. It must all be my imagination...

Age 13

Now on a few antidepressant medications in addition to the initial medication prescribed at age 10, I was fed up with the hassle of taking medication and hated that I "need these meds" according to the psychiatrist.

Honestly, it seemed to me that, somehow, there had to be another option, a better way other than taking medications containing unnatural chemicals. These chemicals caused other symptoms, which I then had to take more medications in order to treat the side effects of the originally prescribed medications. It all seemed like a rather monotonous, vicious cycle.

But I'm not a doctor, so what do I know?

Mother came into my room to tuck me in and handed me my pills, which I then refused to take. "Eliza, you know you can't go without these," she said. "The doctor prescribes them for a reason."

Never having done any research about medications, the dependency they cause, or the side effects (many of which I would experience firsthand later), I replied glumly, "I know."

Doctors wouldn't prescribe medications if they were bad for us. If they caused a lot of long-term side effects or contained harmful chemicals, everyone would know about it. The government wouldn't allow harmful chemicals in medications, which is why they have regulations about what they can put in them, just like they regulate what is allowed to be put in our food.

A few nights later, I went to Mother about yet another instance in which Father had insulted and berated me.

As if it were a ritual, she made the usual excuses for him, "He didn't mean it," and "His daddy walking out on him made it difficult for him to express himself."

I was sick of her excuses for him.

Why was it okay for him to hurt me? Why was it okay for Mother to make excuses for him?

Feeling lower than the slimiest urchin at the bottom of the deepest part of the ocean floor, all of my feelings began to surface. Every feeling I had been afraid to express, each of the feelings that I had expressed to Mother that never were validated, every hurt and rage that I had felt forced to keep bottled deep within my soul, all erupted at once. I couldn't contain the anger any longer. I was so angry. Angry that she wouldn't help me, angry that she allowed him to hurt me, angry about her constant excuses for him, angry that she prioritized him over me. Angry that I was clearly never enough for her.

In a fit of range, I lunged at Mother, subconsciously out of sheer desperation. Unable to express the feelings I was having, as there were way too many to begin to comprehend, all I could manage to do was let out a guttural scream of agony.

I was horrified to see fear in her eyes instead of the empathy and compassion I was seeking.

Feeling like I was both a stranger and a monster to my own mother, I shrank back in disbelief and disappointment.

She's my mother! How could she let him treat me that way? And why was she scared of me? Why can't she hear the agony in my scream? Why did she assume it's a scream of anger? Doesn't she know me at all? Does she really not know she raised me better than that? And why did she have to let it go on until it was too much for me to bear? Her maternal instinct should tell her what I need! She should know without a doubt!

At our next psychiatrist appointment, she recounted this incident to the psychiatrist, again displaying fear and shock.

Feeling again like a hideous monster, I also now felt like such a freak as well. A complete outsider, even to my own family.

She is supposed to be my mother. How could she be scared of me, her own daughter? Or maybe she doesn't think of me that way. I was adopted after all. I've known all along that she has always felt as if she settled for me. I'm not what she really wants. I'm not biologically hers. That's too bad for her, too. A biological child wouldn't be screwed up like I am. That's probably why my birth parents don't want me. They must've sensed that I would be screwed up.

After that incident, the psychiatrist prescribed even more medication, mood stabilizers to "help control the outbursts" and give Mother peace of mind that I wouldn't have another "violent outburst." Yet again, I was force fed those man-made chemicals as a supplement to my daily needs, regardless of how I felt about it. I was not given a choice.

In Math class one day in seventh grade, some boys began launching spit balls at me. The shy, quiet and awkward kid that I was, I was too uncomfortable to stand up for myself, so I tried to ignore it. Much to my surprise, one of the popular girls, Charity, got up from her seat in the middle of the teacher's lesson, walked across the room, and whispered to the boys to stop doing that to me. It surprised me even more when Charity then walked over to me and whispered, "Are you okay?" I peered back at her, taken completely aback that someone, much less someone like Charity, one of the popular girls, actually cared about me, and enough so to actually defend me.

After my initial shock, I replied to her, "Yeah."

Before I could even thank her, she was already headed back to her seat.

Later on that same year in Social Studies, the teacher assigned us a project to do with a partner. Charity was seated at my table, and therefore had to choose between another popular girl or myself to be her partner.

Great! The teacher is letting the head of the table choose their partner. I'm gonna get stuck with the other odd person out, the other outcast like me.

Charity didn't hesitate to choose her partner, announcing to everyone, "I wanna work with Eliza."

I was too shocked to even acknowledge her, as I sat silently in sheer disbelief that someone, a popular girl no less, actually chose me as her partner!

Age 14

On a regular basis, Mother and Father and I went out to dinner with some close family friends, who also had a son just a little bit younger than I. The adults used this time to catch up on monthly happenings with each family, and we two kids used this as time to play games, as we were just along for the ride and really had no choice in the matter.

On this particular occasion, Mother discussed how proud she was of Father, who had been invited to yet another awards ceremony through the school where he was employed.

Mother said, "Paul is getting another award for 'most influential teacher.'"

"Again?" asked one of their friends.

"You just got one last year didn't you?" their other friend questioned.

"Yeah," replied Father. "I was nominated by another student again this year. She said I inspired her much more than any of the other teachers she ever worked with."

For an assignment in English Composition class in eighth grade, the class was given a group assignment during which we had to go over to a classmate's house to create a video. Our group of five kids went over to our classmate Sally's house to complete the assignment. Once we had finished the video, Sally's parents complimented our little group on a job well done, and offered us some light snacks. Sally's father said, "Now that you guys are done with the assignment, you can go over to the neighbor's house and help Sally rake their leaves."

We all laughed, and one of our classmates chimed in, "Yeah, now we'll help you, Sally."

We quickly discovered that her parents weren't actually joking. They told us to bundle up, as it was twenty degrees outside.

Knowing how concerned Mother always was about my allergies, I stated frantically, "I better call my parents and make sure it's okay with them."

"Yeah," chimed in one of my classmates.

"No," countered Sally's Mother, "You can call them once you're done."

Shocked, we all began to realize we had no choice in the matter. So off we went out into the cold, walking through one neighbor's yard to get to the yard of the neighbor in question.

"It's so cold," one of my classmates said.

"I know," I agreed. "I didn't bring my heavier coat because I thought I was only going from the warm car to Sally's house and back."

"Same!" said another classmate.

After about forty five minutes, we finished raking the yard, and walked back to Sally's house. To celebrate a job well done, her parents gave us all hot chocolate.

I remember thinking, *"You jerks better do something for us after forcing us all to do your daughter's work and freeze half to death out there."*

We each left Sally's house around 7:30 in the evening, thus forcing each family to eat a late dinner.

Once safely in the car and out of ear shot, I told Mother what had happened, and how none of us had even been permitted to call our families.

Mother was outraged. "They shouldn't have made you do that, and especially not without my permission! It's too cold for you guys to be out for that long, especially with the way you were dressed in that light jacket. How are you doing with your allergies? Your eyes will be red for days!"

By the time I got home and finished dinner, I was beyond exhausted and ready for bed, however, I had to finish the rest of my homework from my other classes. I didn't get to bed until around midnight that night.

As Mother tucked me in, she expressed her concern for my exhaustion, and again displaying her annoyance with my classmate's parents, saying, "I still can't believe they made you do that! If I was more outgoing, I would probably say something to them!"

The next day, one of my classmates asked Sally, "Did your parents really make you guys rake the leaves?"

"Yeah," she responded. "My parents got so many angry calls that night."

The other classmates laughed.

Sally then turned to me and said, "Your parents are the only ones who didn't complain."

Yeah, because Father doesn't care and Mother is too much of a coward.

I discussed openly in class one of the occasions in which Father had lost his temper again and hit me. I mentioned it casually because I was afraid of becoming too emotional and showing how vulnerable I truly felt.

The teacher whom I mentioned this in front of had previously met him during a parent-teacher night. Because Father was such an excellent actor at feigning empathy, that particular teacher never took my comment seriously.

At that age, I was still so confused on what was really happening to me, yet on some subconscious level, I was slightly aware of the disconnect I felt between myself and my parents. I didn't realize Father was abusive, or that Mother was insecure and afraid, but I no longer felt close to either of them.

I was the weirdo that had only one friend and the uncool dork in school who hugged my teachers. One day, one of my teachers commented on how empathetic I was compared to my classmates, who, unlike me, never bothered to ask the teachers how they were. Then she commented on how sweet I was to hug them all. She said my parents were lucky to have me, and then asked if I hugged them too.

I responded honestly that I didn't. When she asked me why, I said I didn't know. I had honestly never thought about it before.

That was when I realized that I was no longer close to them. Then I began wondering why I felt closer to my teachers, my neighbors, even my other relatives, than my own parents.

I also became obsessed with the thought of meeting and reconnecting with my birth mother, but really had no idea why. Although I no longer still wish to meet her, I realize now that the reason was because of the lovely "the grass is greener on the other side" theory. I had been theorizing that my biological mother wouldn't allow me to be hurt and would defend me if she discovered how I was being treated, unlike my adoptive mother. Really more so hoping, as I subconsciously didn't believe that anyone would want me, much less the person who had already given me up.

Unsure of how to express my desire to my parents, I took to one of my favorite hobbies at the time, writing. I wrote all my feelings out one night, and the following day, showed it to my favorite teacher in private. The teacher agreed to call my mother after school that day to explain to her what I had written and discuss my feelings with her to, as she said, "break the ice a little bit."

That night, my heart raced when the phone rang, because I knew it was my teacher, and knew exactly why she was calling.

After Mother got off the phone, she came into my room as usual to tuck me in. She didn't mention the phone call at all, so my heart continued to thud in my chest as my nerves remained heightened.

After pretending that it was business as usual, I couldn't bear it anymore, so I asked, "Who was on the phone?"

She told me it had been my teacher who had called, and that she claimed that I had seemed a little sad that day.

"Is everything alright?" she then asked.

After several minutes of being dumbfounded, I grew furious. I knew that either my teacher or my mother had lied to me. The problem was that I wasn't sure which person was at fault.

When I questioned the teacher the next day as to what she had discussed with Mother, she said she had discussed the exact nature of what I had written with her. I still didn't know who to believe, although I wanted to believe that neither of them would do me the indecency of lying, especially not directly to my face.

Mother kept up her pretense, and it was driving me mad.

If the teacher had told her, why wasn't she discussing it with me? She always says, "I don't lie," and is terrified of committing any sins. How can she be comfortable lying now? She's really trying to make sure the subject never gets broached!

I knew she would be uncomfortable if I wanted to meet my birth mother, which was why I went to all the trouble of writing it all out and going out of my way to share it with my teacher.

Didn't she know it was really bothering me? Or does she even care?

Almost a week later, I became so uncomfortable that I couldn't bear it anymore. I was too uncomfortable to finish eating dinner, so I finally brought it up.

Afraid to look either of my parents in the eye, I affixed my eyes downward at the dinner table as I mumbled, "I want to meet my birth mom."

Mother had the audacity to say, "What?" forcing me to speak the uncomfortable, painful words again.

She knows damn well what's bothering me. Why the hell is she making me say it again? What a sadist!

It was then that my parents told me that it was against the law for me to even try to reach out to my birth mother until I turned eighteen.

Part of me thought that that seemed like an awfully convenient excuse, and wondered if maybe they weren't being truthful, or that they knew more about my biological family than they were letting on.

But what could I say? What could I do? I have no idea how to go about trying to find her. My parents are the only link I have towards trying to.

I was so disappointed, as I really wanted to meet her. I believed that she would be different from my parents and that, once I told her how they were making me feel, she would rescue me and take me back, just so I would be safe.

Then Father used his manipulative tactics in an attempt to make me lose all desire to ever reach out to her, saying, "You don't need to meet that kind of riff-raff anyway."

Mother scolded him with her usual, "*Paul!*"

As usual, Father ignored her.

"What's riff-raff?" I asked.

"Someone who's not very classy," he replied icily.

"Why is she not very classy?" I questioned, very offended.

"Well," Father continued, "she was very young, and probably not very bright since she didn't finish high school."

I felt insulted by his words so the only thing I could think to do was ask what he meant by that.

He said matter-of-factly, "Anyone who would be having a baby at that young age isn't worth much anyway."

Instantly believing that my biological mother, my supposed saving grace, was not a good person, and believing that if I shared genes with a person, that made me who I was, I was overwhelmed. Unsure of what to do with that or how to react, I ran to my bedroom and sobbed intensely. I continued to do so for the rest of the night, eventually crying myself to sleep for the first of many times to come.

Father later escalated things further by making it a point to tell the people he associated with that I had been adopted, and that my biological mother had been "too young to really be a parent." He also would tell people that my biological father was a drug addict, a theory that Mother had even admitted in therapy had been suspected but was never proven.

Finding out that I was biologically related to a drug addict was also quite difficult for me to comprehend at that young age, as I had yet to realize that biology doesn't define who you are or who you will become. At that time, I was still under the impression that the people you are biologically related to somehow shape you. I was honestly ashamed to share DNA and a bloodline with someone who had a problem like that.

Father wouldn't talk down about someone if the problem they had was acceptable. Obviously, being an addict is a very bad thing that only can happen to the weak and disgusting.

Funny how at that young age I was never able to realize that Father's cigarette smoking and Mother's codependency made both of them addicts. Father was a cigarette addict, and Mother was addicted to people and to not being alone. I would not realize until later that they had passed those traits down to me, thus making me an addict as well.

On the last day of eighth grade, the majority of the students in my math class had become quite rowdy. Clearly driving the teacher nuts, she decided to bring order to the students by leading us all in a game.

"I'm going to walk around the room, and when I place my hand over each student's head, the class will all say that person's name."

She started on the left side, making her way toward the back of the first row, then the front of the second row, then the back of the third row, and so on, to reach each student in the order they had been seated in. Everyone was doing a great job of reciting each student's name, as we had all been in school together an entire year, so we'd had an entire school year to get to know everyone's name.

The teacher reached me last, as I had been seated in the front row.

Having been in the front row all year with a teacher who liked to call on all students equally, people will at least know my name finally. I'm usually unpopular, so this will be a nice change of pace for once.

As the teacher placed her hand over my head, however, everyone sat there dumbfounded.

It was then that I realized I wasn't unpopular at all. Much worse, I was basically invisible. The long pause the teacher gave the class before finally enlightening the class of the name of the invisible dork who had been in the front row the entire school year didn't help. I was completely embarrassed and utterly ashamed of who I was: nobody.

I was already all but nobody at home, and now I was nobody at school, too.

If I suddenly died in a car crash today, no one would miss me except Mother.

Age 15

Mother started going to the doctor for her frequent headaches, which eventually became a daily issue that severely affected her to the point that she was unable to do anything except lie down and rest. They would run tests on her periodically for the next several years but would never find any physical cause for them. It wasn't until I discovered a book about how verbal abuse and psychological gaslighting makes a person feel chronically sick that I fully comprehended why Mother and I rarely ever felt well.

I was in high school at this point. The building was bigger, the halls much more crowded, and I was that much more invisible. I was thankful to have my one and only friend, Rose. Having Rose was great, and much better than having no one.

Even still, I longed for more social interaction. I hadn't seen Charity much since seventh grade, and never ran into her, even throughout eighth grade and freshman year. Her kindness stuck with me though, and she entered my mind on several occasions throughout those years, to the point that I found myself wishing to run into her. I missed her, which was odd to me because I really didn't know her well at all. I held out hope that someday I would see her again, and we could get to know each other and become close friends, as she seemed just like the kind hearted person I needed in my life, like Rose.

Age 16

School was so difficult, both socially and academically. I still had only one friend and wasn't smart enough to do well with anything I attempted to learn, or so I believed. Due to the constant insults and curses I received at home, I was afraid to even try for fear that I would get the answers wrong.

This inferiority complex also caused me to be terrified to even attempt to obtain my driver's license.

What was the point? I can't do anything right, so why even try? Besides, the last thing the world needs is someone like me who's an inferior being on the road and endangering everyone's lives.

Regardless of how many times I told Father "No, I will never drive," he continued to pressure me about it constantly.

Looking back now, I see clearly that he just wanted me out of the house and out of his way.

My home life was growing increasingly worse. In addition to being berated, threatened, and controlled, Father had decided to start discussing his feelings about Mother with me directly. I heard countless times about how "lazy" she was for asking us to help her carry the groceries inside, and how annoyed he was that he frequently had to help her do things.

He discussed with me their finances, showing me that she had more money than he did in her bank account. He told me that he wanted to buy me the things I wanted, but "*Mom* thinks you should have to *work* for it, but *I* don't think that's right when you're so busy with school."

He was an expert at playing us against each other, and the problem was that he knew it. He had accomplished his goal of turning me against her. God only knows what horrible things he was telling her that I had supposedly said behind her back. It's no wonder that she came to view him as her confidante. Looking back now, I can just imagine him putting words in my mouth, telling her all of the horrible things that I had supposedly said about her. Then I'm sure he convinced her that he would never say anything about her behind her back, and that the two of them should work together as a parental unit, and should therefore discuss everything about me with each other.

This same year, right before Christmas time, Father received a package in the mail, telling us it was from a former student. It contained a box of chocolates, along with a heartfelt note written on a Christmas card.

"That was so sweet," Father announced to Mother and I. "She wrote me a letter thanking me for being such an influential part of her life during high school. She even told me that I was like the Father figure she's never had. Apparently her father wasn't around much, and when he was he wasn't very nice to her most of the time.

That was the first year that that particular former student sent him a gift. She proceeded to send a gift and heartfelt card to him every Christmas afterward.

Wow, I must have a really neat Dad! Most people don't get gifts from people they don't even see much anymore. I guess I'm pretty lucky to have him as a Dad.

Age 17

Happily the king of his kingdom, Father had us both where he wanted us. Neither Mother nor I realized that we could do anything about Father's manipulation or insults.

Once, he even went so far as to share a joke he read one day.

"Listen to this," he exclaimed. "Man proposed to woman, woman said no, and man lived happily ever after."

After chuckling, he looked directly at me and said, "It's true!"

I didn't think it was very nice, but I found it sweet that Father was so close to me. After all, Mother had been saying things about me behind my back (which I believed at the time thanks to Father's clever manipulations). Plus, he always called me his "girl" and bought me things from time to time, if we could afford it. Of course, the drawback was that there were always strings attached.

But what could I do? I'm not bringing in any money of my own. And my anxiety keeps getting worse, so getting a job after high school doesn't look like a possibility.

Having been berated and controlled at home so much had hardened me to the point that I had become hateful and angry. I hated people and wanted to be left alone. I hated how emotional Mother often was and thought much less of her for displaying her emotions. The reading assignments I had to do for Language Arts class were filled with emotional recounting of various characters or authors. Reading about all those emotions disgusted me, even the uplifting narratives.

This shit is so corny! This author is such a pussy! Why do they always have to sugar coat this emotional bullshit?

I had become emotionally dead inside, aside from the harmful, negative emotions such as hatred, rage, judgment, etc.

One school day, I came home enraged and disgusted.

Father asked me, "What happened? Why are you so mad?"

I recounted what had happened, saying, "On the bus, this dumb guy decided to be gross and spit out the window, but because the bus was moving, his fucking spit wad flew right back inside the bus and onto my face!"

Without hesitation, Father began laughing hysterically, despite my obvious disgust and frustration.

What the fuck! I'm glad my torture of getting germs spit on me is so amusing to your asshole self!

The social outcast that I was, I really didn't resonate with people my own age, so I had befriended my bus driver. Unlike everyone else, she actually saw me and I wasn't invisible to her. Plus she was fun to talk to, which was an added bonus.

She eventually confided in me that she had never finished high school, and that she would "give anything to go back." She made it a point to tell me to do my homework each night, which I honestly wasn't going to do. But because I didn't want to disappoint my newfound friend, I decided to do as she had requested, even though I really didn't want to.

Age 18

School was not just hard for me socially, it was also hard academically, as I was always afraid of doing things incorrectly and getting answers wrong. Hearing mostly insults and curses at home and believing I was nothing but a disappointment who couldn't do anything right made me believe that school was pointless for me.

I barely get passing grades, its so hard for me socially and academically, and I will never go to college since I can't do anything right. There's no future for someone like me who isn't good at anything. So what's the point of continuing with school? It'll be better for my mental health, and will also save Mother and Father a bunch of money that would otherwise be wasted.

Mother and Father had been discussing things we would have to get for the coming school year, which made me extremely uneasy, as I had decided to drop out of school. I knew that at some point soon, I would have to tell them, so I decided to take the bandage approach--I would do it instantly and quickly.

They reacted as I knew they would, angry, disappointed, but not necessarily surprised as I had voiced to them during previous years that I had considered dropping out, to which they had replied, "You can't make decisions without parental permission until you're 18." They, and their friends as well, tried several times to persuade me not to, but I've never been one to cave under pressure, so their attempts failed. Eventually, they enlisted the aid of one of my teachers, who called the house to try and persuade me not to.

"You're parents tell me that you're very seriously considering not coming back and joining us this year," she said.

Unashamedly, I responded, "That's right."

After several long minutes of listening to the teacher list the many benefits of a high school diploma as well as the drawback of not having one, I couldn't help but think of Lisa. I began thinking about what she does for a living, and how she's had to have two jobs at times. Then I asked myself if I thought Lisa was happy doing what she does for a living. And then her exact words began echoing through my mind, "I'd give anything to go back."

One of my biggest fear in life at that time was the fear of regret. I realized that what is done can not be undone, and that if I dropped out I would have to complete my schooling all over again, even the years I had already completed. Time is our most precious commodity, and unless I completed high school, the previous three years would be wasted.

Even though this next year might be a waste, it better than realizing later that I wasted three of them instead of just one.

With that, I decided to stick it out, and not drop out of high school.

One morning during my senior year of high school, I was walking down the hallways when suddenly I noticed a group of girls sobbing profusely. This was odd to me, yet I really didn't think much of it other than rolling my eyes at them exposing their vulnerability, which I perceived as weakness.

A few minutes later, I noticed that a teacher was talking with that group of girls quite intently, her face displaying more than the usual amount of concern. It was almost as if something quite serious had occurred.

Well, whatever it is, I don't need to know. It's none of my business anyway.

Immediately after the bell rang to announce the start of first period, the principal came over the school's loudspeaker. I knew right away something was odd, as announcements were always made in the afternoon, as the school day concluded, but never in the morning as soon as school began.

"Good morning students. As many of you know, there was an auto accident that occurred late last night that took the life of one of our own."

This was news to me, which wasn't surprising given my extreme unpopularity. Yet it did come as a bit of a shock, given that high school age isn't very old, especially not old enough to die yet. Nevertheless I drowned most of the rest of the announcement out, cold and unfeeling as I had become. That is, until the principal gave the student's name.

"We will forever hold the life of Charity Barnes in our hearts."

Too surprised for words or emotions, I went about the rest of my day as usual.

I really didn't know her well anyway.

I even remember recounting the announcement to my bus driver as if it was nothing more than gossip.

That night after dinner, however, reality finally sunk in and emotion washed over me like a shit ton of bricks. I had finally comprehended that Charity was gone. I understood that I really hadn't even known her, but for some reason I grew extremely upset at her passing.

I began sobbing profusely and uncontrollably. I was in disbelief, but had finally come to comprehend what happened.

What the fuck? Oh God, no! Not Charity. Not sweet Charity. Why?! Why did this happen? And to such a great, amazing person?

That was the first time in years that I had actually allowed myself to show emotion, even privately, away from everyone else. For the life of me, I couldn't figure out why the death of someone I had barely known had caused my emotional floodgates to open, and so heavily.

In hindsight I realize that it was because Charity had been like my protector. On some level deep within me I was aware of this. Even my own mother had never protected me.

My one and only protector had died. She had been taken from me, and from now on I was left to fend for myself.

Isolating myself for the past several years led me to feel safe within the walls of my home, a safety I had become afraid to leave. It had been years since I had actually left the house to go out with anyone other than my small handful of friends.

In addition to isolation, I had resorted to consuming excess amounts of comfort food in order to cope with the immense emotional pain I was constantly in. Because of this unhealthy lifestyle change, I had gained a decent amount of weight as compared to the skinny person I had always been before. At this point, I was chubby, so I figured that no one would want to be with me romantically. After all, it was evident from Father's frequent put downs and constant disappointment in me that I could never do anything right.

So what is the point in even trying? I'm ugly anyway, and obviously can't do anything right.

I had made the stereotypical mistake of giving up on myself because everyone around me had already done so.

If I mattered, then someone would care that Father doesn't treat me well and would stand up for me.

One night, some neighbors invited me to tag along with them to a live music and dinner event that took place outside our local bar and grill. Jumping at a chance to finally be included in something, I took my neighbors up on their offer.

There was an acquaintance that one of them knew who was also there, and he seemed to be taking an interest in me. I was flattered, but guessed that if he got to know me, he probably wouldn't even like me. It must just be my slightly pretty, albeit chubby, face that made him interested.

We went on about the night, had dinner, and enjoyed the live music. My neighbor's acquaintance even agreed to teach me how to sing, which I was very excited about.

It was a typical night out on the town, so to speak...until I had to go to the bathroom. The bathroom was inside the bar, and I was allowed to pass through the bar even though I wasn't legally old enough to be inside. On my way out of the bar, an acquaintance approached me.

Within seconds, I realized he had partaken of one too many, as he was tipsy as he conversed with me. He asked me if I wanted to go out sometime, and, terrified of confrontation, I said, "Sure."

Besides, I was assuming that he wouldn't remember it the next day given how much he had had to drink.

Before I knew it, he had me cornered against a wall and, in less than the blink of an eye, had forced his tongue into my mouth.

I was so disgusted and uncomfortable but not physically strong enough to push him away. I looked around the bar, hoping that just one person would notice the situation and help me out, especially since I was a minor. I observed a bartender chatting with a patron, both of whom were male.

My terrified, helpless eyes met theirs, and I knew that I didn't need words, as the situation was clearly unsafe to any untrained eye. However, not wanting to be involved with such a messy situation, they both instantly looked away and pretended nothing bad or wrong was happening.

I was shocked and horrified beyond comprehension.

Fucking cowards! How dare you!

It was apparent that I was completely on my own, with no one there to defend me. What's worse, I was helpless due to lack of physical strength.

I was desperately trying to figure a way out of the situation. My first thought was to bite the guy's tongue, but realized it wasn't worth it to have a random, disgusting person's blood in my mouth in addition to the repulsive tongue, saliva, and who knew how much bacteria that was already in there.

After a few minutes that seemed to stretch on much longer, he finally tipsied himself away from me, and I bolted out of the bar faster than I had ever moved before.

Embarrassed at what happened and feeling weak both physically and mentally, I was afraid to mention it to my neighbors.

We rode home together with the two of them conversing, but I remained silent, still trying to process the frightful turn of events.

I felt violated yet again and believed that I had been stupid not to have realized that the man was a pariah.

This is all my fault! I'm so ashamed... Someone has to be drunk to find me *desirable.*

"A skunk walked into a bar..." You're telling me! I met the skunk personally. Instead of walking into that bar, I guess I should've ducked. Of course, I ended up playing metaphorical limbo either way.

Years later, I would discover that that particular man was actually the husband of a friend of mine, who she would later end up divorcing.

Age 19

Never resonating with people my own age, I had befriended my teachers and also my bus driver Lisa while in high school, and had kept in touch with all of them afterward. One day, I told Mother that I missed seeing Lisa, as I hadn't seen her in a while.

Mother, who really didn't have many friends, seemed quite jealous that I was focusing on someone other than her, responding with, "Why are you so focused on seeing her? You usually only spend time with Rose."

"Because I haven't seen her lately," I responded. "I got to see some of my teachers since high school, but haven't seen her."

"Do you want to go see her now?" asked Mother.

"What do you mean?" I asked.

"School recently let out," she replied. "Why don't I drive you over to the bus lot and you can see her."

Something about this suggestion didn't feel right, but who was I to question someone older and wiser than I?

Mother and I got in the car, and she drove me to the bus lot, where we found out that Lisa was on a field trip that night, and wouldn't be back for another hour or so.

"Do you know what school she is doing the field trip for?" Mother questioned.

"Yeah," I replied.

"Which one is it? We'll go there so you can see her." said Mother.

I had officially grown very uncomfortable. "I don't know if that's such a good idea."

"Why not?" Mother questioned.

"That's kind of intrusive isn't it?" I asked.

Just then, a police officer drove up to our vehicle, as he found it odd that a random vehicle would be parked near the school bus lot after hours.

Mother gasped as she noticed the officer standing outside her vehicle.

"Is everything okay here?" the police officer asked Mother.

Appearing extremely nervous, she said, "I'm sorry officer. My daughter was trying to see her bus driver friend, but she's not here, so we were about to leave."

"No worries," responded the police officer casually.

After the officer drove off, Mother started the car again and drove off the lot, heading in a direction opposite of the way home.

"Where are we going?" I questioned.

"To see your friend!" she responded. "Where do you think?"

"I told you we should just go home," I was growing increasingly nervous.

"E-li-za! There was a police officer that approached my door!" she yelled frantically. I am most certainly not going to go home after I told the officer we were going to see your friend!"

Why is she wigging out over a calm and collected police officer checking in on us when we've done nothing wrong?

Once we got to the school where Lisa was supposed to be, I was petrified to see that her bus was still in the parking lot. I had been hoping that she would have left by then. Going out of the way to find her in a place she wouldn't normally be felt extremely stalky to me.

"Well," Mother prompted. "We drove all this way. Go ahead and see her."

I will never forget that night and how uncomfortable Lisa was to see me randomly showing up.

"What are you doing here?" she asked. "How did you get here?"

"My mom drove me," I said, trying to sound like this was no big deal, but realizing that this was far from normal.

"You shouldn't be here," Lisa said. "Go home."

Embarrassed to say anymore, and realizing that Mother had more than likely ruined this relationship, I immediately left.

"That was quick," said Mother as I got back to the car.

When I said nothing more, she asked, "How did it go?"

"She said I shouldn't be here," I responded, trying in the back of my mind to forget that I had attempted to tell Mother what a bad idea this was.

"That wasn't very nice," she responded.

Although I realized that this was far from normal, I chose to believe that Mother's actions that night really weren't that strange.

Her heart is in the right place. She's just different than most people. She meant well, although I really hope this doesn't ruin my relationship with Lisa.

Early the next morning, the phone rang, caller ID indicating that it was originating from the local school system.

I wondered instantly if it was about Lisa.

Upon hanging up, I questioned Mother, "Who was it?"

"It was from Lisa's work." She wore a puzzled expression as she said, "They said Lisa was very upset from that visit last night. "What happened? Did you say something to her?"

I was dumbfounded.

When later recounting this incident to my therapist in a joint session with Mother, the therapist asked Mother why she had driven me to see her unannounced, and why she had taken me to try to locate her after the fieldtrip.

"I don't know," Mother responded. "It was like Eliza really wanted to see this person."

"I don't know that I would've gone to her place of employment," said the therapist, "especially without any advanced notice."

"No?" Mother responded, embarrassed. "I guess given that Lisa was upset, it wasn't the right thing to do."

Ya think? I tried to tell you, and now I have lost one of my only friends because of you!

I attempted to get the help I needed by letting a close friend of the family know that, "Behind closed doors, things are happening that shouldn't be" and that that was the reason for my wanting to kill myself.

The response she offered was, "Stop exaggerating. You know that's not *really* happening. And stop saying you wanna die. You know it's not *that* bad."

I was completely stunned. Here was this close friend of the family, who had been in our lives for many years, and who always stated that, "...since I know Eliza so well."

Yeah, right! Doesn't anybody know me at all? Why does everyone think I'm so horrible that I would make things up? Lying is my biggest pet peeve because it's what Father does all the time!

Knowing that Father would enter the passcode on my phone and take the liberty of scrolling through my photos and reading my text messages was just a normal part of my life. Being asked to reset my phone because the tracker wasn't showing my location was, I assumed, what all parents did.

But now I was at the age where it was starting to bother me, yet I knew that I didn't dare express it. Expressing it was asking for a world of trouble. I also knew my independence was forbidden, but what could I do about it? After all, Father often made me realize my limitations, saying, "You can't work full time. You'll run yourself into the ground!" And I had grown up hearing, "You can't do that," countless times.

Regardless, I one day decided to keep private a conversation I had had between my best friend and I. Father later asked what we had been talking about, and I stated simply that it had been a private conversation that she had asked me not to share with anyone. He poked and prodded me as usual, but I refused to budge, thus making him even more frustrated with me.

This was just the start of several times that I would keep things to myself, to which Father would always ask, "Why do you always have to be so secretive?"

It wasn't my intent to be. I just wanted some sort of independence in my life without him always prying into it as if he needed to know my every move, thought, and intention.

One year, our family figured out that the Robbins next door were having problems, as evident by the ambulance and police vehicles that would periodically appear at their residence. A very warm, open, and honest family, they later confided in us that their son had become addicted to drugs (something that I would later discover firsthand is usually caused by prescription medication) and that one of their daughters was struggling with self-mutilation.

Mother's reaction was that of sympathy, saying, "That poor family."

Father, on the other hand, met them with judgement and disgust, saying, "God damn it! Not again. They're going to bring our property values down!"

The Robbins had been living next door to us for several years, and had become like a second family to me, which was why I didn't appreciate Father's derogatory, hateful comments towards them. As a matter of fact, it made me angrier at him. It was bad enough that he was so horrible to me.

And now he's talking shit about my other family! He acts like he's so above them, but does he really think he's all that?

Age 20

For my grandparent's wedding anniversary, they had asked everyone to make the voyage across state lines so all the kids and grandkids could be there to celebrate with them.

Father complained openly around Mother and I about having to go around the holidays, yet kept telling Grandma, "It's okay, we don't mind. You're not ruining our holiday."

Because we were going to be away on Christmas Day, Father told us we would celebrate our Christmas a few days prior. I had asked Mother if Rose could spend the night that night, and somehow misunderstood her. I thought she had okayed it, but something had apparently gotten lost in translation, as when I brought up that Rose and I would like to have rolls for breakfast, Mother grew quite upset.

"I told you Rose couldn't spend the night! The fact that you would deliberately disobey me and invite her over anyway is unacceptable. We are *very* disappointed in you!"

Taken aback, I responded, "I didn't deliberately disobey you. I thought you said she *could* stay?"

"I most certainly did not, and you know I did not." Mother responded coldly. "Again, we are *very* disappointed in you!"

Her scorn hit me like scolding hits a puppy dog who's only mission is to please his master.

Doesn't anybody know me at all?

About a week later, we were making our way back from my grandparents' house. We were driving through Tennessee when traffic became congested and eventually we became gridlocked in bumper to bumper traffic. Mother busied herself with a magazine, and I with my music, my faithful relatability as well as my escape.

Suddenly, the vehicle jolted as we heard a crash as well as stuttering thuds.

Mother gasped, as was her usual reaction to anything and everything unexpected, and I looked up startled.

Father appeared quite disoriented, as well as rather out of sorts.

"What happened?" questioned Mother.

Without hesitation, Father instantly replied, "I think I fell asleep."

Mother's jaw dropped as Father immediately exited the vehicle to speak to the driver of the vehicle that ours had just collided with.

I couldn't believe my ears. *Did Father just admit to something? He never shows any vulnerability or admits any fault!*

After talking for a few minutes, Father reentered the vehicle, which was quite difficult as the driver door had been smashed to the point that the door would no longer fully open.

Before Mother or I could say anything else, Father then said, "Did you see the licence plate of the car that cut me off?"

"No!" Mother immediately responded. "What happened?"

"This guy in a gray SUV came into my lane so I had to swerve into the other lane to avoid him. That's why I hit the van in front of us."

Soon, a police officer arrived at the scene to assess the situation and file a report. After he spoke to everyone, he dismissed the occupants of the other vehicle from the scene, but told Father to wait there for a minute.

After several minutes, Father said, "He's taking his sweet time, isn't he?"

The officer eventually exited his vehicle and returned to Father's door, handing him back his licence and registration. The officer then explained to him that he had also issued him a ticket for following too closely.

"In bumper to bumper traffic?" Father questioned the officer.

At the time, I had been easily fooled, just like Mother, into completely forgetting that he had admitted he had fallen asleep and only remembered the story he had created about the supposed other driver of an SUV.

Looking back now, I find it stupid of Father to even question the officer, who had obviously been trained in accident trajectory as part of the job.

After pulling away from the scene, Father showed his disgust at the officer's discipline of him, saying "What a dumbass! How can I help following too closely? It's bumper to bumper traffic! He's got it out for me. He was taking his sweet time sitting in there on his fat ass!"

Later, Father recounted this story, as he always did, to every one of his associates who would undoubtedly share his view of the incident.

His brother, who had seen us pulled over at the side of the road on his way back home with us, offered to have his daughter, a Tennessee native, contest the officer's story on his behalf.

Realizing that he wouldn't stand a chance as the officer had clearly caught him in a lie, Father told his brother not to have her bother with it.

"Why not?" his brother questioned.

"What's done is done," Father responded. "Besides, I don't want to put your daughter on the spot."

"She wouldn't mind," his brother continued.

"It would be his word against hers, and I don't want to put her through that." Father countered. Still sensing resistance, he added, "Anyway, it's not her fight to fight."

"You shouldn't have to pay that ticket," his brother continued.

Taking brotherly charge, Father sternly said, "George, what's done is done. Just leave it alone. It's not worth the hassle."

By now, I had tried to do as Mother had asked and accept that Father's two-faced comments behind everyone's back was "just who he was," yet it really didn't sit well with me. I didn't understand why someone would keep up such pretense in front of everyone he claimed were his friends.

How could he say he's their friend, yet say such horrible comments about all of them behind their backs? And wasn't faking his personality in front of everyone he didn't live with exhausting? What was the point of it? And how could someone be so cold-hearted? And how had he managed to keep it a secret for so long? How had someone not begun to see the truth by now?

I could tolerate most of his comments, although I wished he would stop lying to everybody. His constant negative opinions of them made it obvious that he was hiding what he really thought. One night, however, he made a comment that disgusted me to my core. That was when I first began to revile him.

An ambulance was again dispatched to the Robbins' house, which we noticed as we peered out our front window at the flashing lights.

It became apparent that Father had had his fill of these events, as he said about their son Ben, "What a waste."

Mother gave her stereotypical, useless scold, "*Paul!*"

Nonetheless, he continued, "And they should just shoot Cathy."

I absolutely could not believe Father's heartlessness, openly displaying a snarl on my face at him.

How could he be so cold behind their backs, yet portray such warmness to their faces? If the Robbins' had any idea that Father was so cruel, they wouldn't bother with him. No one would if they could only see his true colors.

I knew right then and there that I had to be more careful from now on. I already had a knife in my room, which I had been using to make little practice cuts on my skin.

As angry as he is, he probably already has a gun hidden somewhere in the house. If he finds my knife or sees any cuts on me, or if I piss him off, he'll probably shoot me!

Age 21

My parents and I went out to lunch one day where I encountered an old friend from junior high school. It had been some time since we had seen each other, so we agreed to get together soon and catch up.

A few days later, she invited me over to her and her boyfriend's house, which I discussed with my parents over dinner one night. They okayed it, Father even saying that he was glad I was actually being social for once, and saying about my former classmate, "She's weird, but I like her."

The next day, they dropped me off at her apartment. I wasn't there long before an uncomfortable situation arose. She and her boyfriend pulled some weed out of a drawer and were about to smoke it, telling me that I should have some. Since I really wasn't happy and wanted anything to make the pain go away, I considered it very seriously but ultimately decided not to. I was afraid that the weed might linger and that it would be evident to my parents that I had smoked some. I was extremely nervous, but didn't know how to handle confrontation, thanks to the examples set by Mother. I faked that I had a stomach ache, and told my classmate that I was going for a walk outside, but unfortunately she followed me. Then I called Mother, but her phone had been on silent mode, so she didn't pick up.

I can't believe she's unreachable to me. This is an emergency! I need help and she isn't available. Mothers are always supposed to be available.

Yet again, I was asking, *Where is her maternal instinct? If she is so close to me, like she said, how could she not sense what I needed?*

Knowing that Father would feel put out having to come back and get me, I called him anyway. Unlike Mother, he was always reachable (I realize now this was a part of his ploy), so of course he answered my call. I told him he had to come get me because I was feeling sick to my stomach, a pretense I had to continue due to my classmate still standing next to me.

Right on cue, his annoyance was evident. "God damn it, Eliza! We just got back home!"

"I'm sorry," my voice pleaded. "I just *really* don't feel well at all, and *need* to come home, *now*."

"God damn it, Eliza," Father continued on. "Can't you just suck it up for a little bit?"

"Dad, please," I begged.

I was hoping he would figure out by my phrasing it this way and the hesitation between words that there was more to the story than I was letting on, and would realize there was a deeper concern.

"Just...trust me," I said.

Still thoroughly annoyed, he didn't seem to pick up on my hint, but eventually agreed nonetheless. I believe his agreement was more so he wouldn't have to continue the conversation and less because he realized there was a problem.

I knew he would put up a fuss, but thought all of that would change once he and Mother picked me up.

Once I tell him what was going on and that I didn't use any drugs, he'll change his tone. He'll apologize for acting put out and then be so proud of me for making a good decision when I could've gotten away with a bad one behind his back. Finally, I'll earn brownie points with him.

Still heavily annoyed, he and Mother arrived. Once I was in the car and safely out of earshot of my former classmate, I told them both what had actually transpired.

To my shock and horror, Father didn't hesitate as he responded with, "God damn it, Eliza! You should've known that she would do that!"

Completely dumbfounded, I had nothing I could even say. Or even wanted to. I was absolutely speechless. I rode the rest of the way home in silence, realizing that I could never win, no matter what I did.

It's like the expression he always says, "damned if ya do, damned if ya don't." And everyone who "knows us so well" doesn't understand why I have absolutely no self-confidence?! I wonder why that is!!

I felt destined to always be a disappointment no matter how hard I tried. Nothing I ever did was good enough, and I then came to realize on some level that it never would be, at least not in Father's eyes. Or Mother's, otherwise she wouldn't always take his side with everything.

I'm not good enough. I'm not good at all. I can't do anything right, so why try?

As I had been struggling in many different ways, especially when it came to holding down a job, Father and Mother had decided to take the suggestion of a teacher I had had in high school. The teacher had suggested they hire a job coach to help with my anxiety so I could successfully become part of the working world.

Father called me into his office one day to have me apply my signature to the paper for the application of job coaching services. I was so excited to finally get the help I needed that I signed the paper immediately, to which Father was surprised.

He later commented about his surprise to Mother, who equally shared his surprise.

I told them, "It's not that I don't want to work, I just don't know how with anxiety that's so bad."

Yet again, for the millionth time: Does anyone even know me at all?!! What? Do they think I'm some lazy piece of shit that just wants to live off of them? Don't they know how much seeing my classmates on social media all have money to go out and do things tortures me? What kind of person wants to sit around the house all day anyway?

Later, well into my work with the job coaching company, the job coach said to me, "I have a job that might not be so bad for you with your autism."

I paused, taken aback, replying, "I'm not autistic."

"Then why are you using our services?" asked the job coach.

"Because I have severe anxiety," I told her honestly.

She looked as if she didn't believe me, responding, "We don't help with that."

"The teacher from my high school said you did," I responded.

It didn't occur to me until years later that Father had probably told the teacher the same lie he told most people about my supposed autism. It didn't help people believe otherwise that I would ride public transportation to work. Most people living in our county were quite well off, so the public transportation was used mostly by special needs people who couldn't drive. Because of this, there was no need for regular sized buses, so public transportation used short buses only, each with a chair lift to assist a special needs person when needed.

Another reason the job coach believed I was autistic was because I would frequently say, "I can't do that." She mistook that comment, as many did, as lack of confidence in my own abilities. In reality, it was a phrase Father would say to me anytime I discussed working full time or becoming a published author, or moving out or wanting to do anything that cost money.

Age 22

Yet another factor shattering my beliefs about myself was Father's frequent complaints.

On a regular basis, either Mother or myself would suffer from feeling sick, the cause of which I would later discover was his abuse. Our frequent illnesses were well known by all acquaintances of the family, during which time Father would bring us meals in bed, bring us medicine throughout the day, and take one of us to the doctor when needed. We were told by outsiders things like, "He's a really good guy." "You're lucky to have him." "He takes such good care of you." While from all outside perspectives this seemed true, no one could've expected the harsh reality that was transpiring behind closed doors.

Father would say to me behind Mother's back, "I don't get to do anything that I wanna do because I'm always busy taking care of her." I now assume that since we were both frequently sick, he must've been saying the same thing about me to Mother whenever I wasn't around.

While he acted bothered about having to constantly care for us, it quickly became evident that he liked the attention and praise he was getting from friends of the family. Anytime the caller ID showed someone he recognized, Father would answer the phone, saying, "Paul's Infirmary. How can I be of service?"

What family and friends found hilarious was, in reality, my own personal hell. The worst part was that no one would believe me. Always being too sick to work meant that escape was obviously a complete impossibility for me. I realized there was nothing I could do. I knew I was stuck in that situation.

Father informed Mother and I that one of his former students had reached out to him wanting to reconnect. He had made plans with this student to meet at a local restaurant, and then invited me to tag along.

"She's a really neat lady," he told me. "I had her in class about twelve years ago. I think you'll really like her, Eliza."

The next week, when we met with this student, Father introduced us, and we shook hands.

"It's nice to meet you, Eliza," she said. "I've heard a lot of great things about you."

That comment took me completely by surprise. "You have?"

She nodded.

Wow. Why would Father say nice things to her about me? She must just be saying that. It's clear that Father hates me by the way he puts me down and insults me constantly.

The rest of that meeting went on as usual, yet I couldn't help but wonder why she had said that.

Does everyone really not realize that Father is completely different behind closed doors, and that he treats me horribly? Is he really this good at putting on heirs? He really does have everyone fooled!

Mother and I had been frequenting garage sales, and on one occasion, we stumbled upon two pieces of beautifully carved wooden loveseats.

"I love the wood carvings!" I exclaimed to Mother, who instantly agreed. "I really want one of those couches for my room, but I really don't like the fabric. The colors are kind of ugly."

"Well, if they'll take twenty dollars less for one of them," suggested Mother, "then we can reupholster it with fabric you like."

After taking a few seconds to consider, I decided I liked the idea, then Mother said, "Make sure they don't have a funny smell."

Once the owners of the sale weren't looking, I inconspicuously sniffed the material, then nodded to Mother, signifying to her that they were clean of any foul odor. Then I proceeded to give my offer to the owners, who upon consideration, accepted.

A few weeks later, after I had picked out and purchased the fabric I wanted, Mother went to work measuring and sewing. The following day, we removed the staples from the loveseat, and enlisted Father's aid. Mother had the sewing skills, but Father had the equipment we needed to reattach the fabric. Father brought the staple gun up to my room, where we were ready to attach the new fabric.

It had been a while since the last time he had used the staplegun, so he took a moment to be reacquainted with it. He pressed the lever to disengage the staple, thinking it was aimed toward the floor. Instead, however, Mother let out a startled scream, then shouted, "Paul!"

Father and I looked up at Mother, confused, as she had appeared to shout for no reason.

"It hit my hair!" exclaimed Mother, still in shock.

Apparently, he had confused the back end of the staplegun with the end the staples launched from.

I was extremely grateful that the staple had not actually struck Mother. *That would've been really bad! It hit her hair! She's lucky it didn't hit her in the face!*

"It hit your hair?" asked Father.

"Yes!" exclaimed Mother, still frightened and now very much annoyed.

It was clear that Father didn't share the same sentiment as Mother and I, for he immediately began laughing.

All I could think was *Wow*, as I rolled my eyes aloud, taken aback by his complete lack of concern for his own wife.

I really didn't even know what to do with that, or how to process Father's lack of empathy and concern for the woman who was not just his wife, but the mother of his daughter, who had witnessed the whole display.

Age 23

The family dynamics I was raised in were, obviously, interesting to say the least. My father's controlling manipulative behavior and my mother's insecurities, fear, and overly devout religion were apparent to me. Also obvious was the extended family's complete oblivion to what was really occurring.

My grandma was notorious for her so-called rose colored glasses within the family, as two of her sons didn't really get along with the third one. This was well known, yet it was only discussed behind everyone's backs (except Grandma and Grandpa's), so everyone would force pretense to get along during family gatherings. If Grandma had an opinion about what someone was doing, or the way a person was doing it, she wouldn't hesitate to tell them so directly. I found her to be rather harsh for a grandmother, and her comments were slightly reminiscent of my father's derogatory opinions of others, yet not nearly as bad. Grandma's comments were more critical, whereas Father's were downright insulting.

My grandpa, on the other hand, was an argumentative man, but could take it or leave it. He would always let bygones be bygones, so to speak, and never harbored any grudges. He was by far more empathetic and discerning than anyone else in the family. He always knew how to make a person feel their best, contrary to my grandmother.

Because of Grandma's criticisms, Grandpa was my favorite, although I always felt guilty even admitting such a thing, even to myself.

There were certain times when I had wondered what Grandpa had seen in her. It was well known within the family that Grandma had had an affair while Grandpa had been away in the armed forces.

This was a weird dynamic to me from the moment I found out. Honestly, I resented my grandmother for having done that to Grandpa. To this day, I have no idea if he ever knew about the affair or not.

Grandma and Grandpa lived far away across several state lines, so I didn't see them much, and when I did, it was a big treat for me. Most of the time, seeing them meant they traveled to see us, rarely the other way around.

Father would always make the financial excuse, claiming that it cost a lot of money to come see them. In reality, he didn't want to be bothered. He loved doing what he wanted to do, and hated that every time we went down to see them he was "put to work" washing the house, cleaning the gutters, and doing other things of that nature. The fact that his elderly parents shouldn't be doing those things didn't seem to matter to him. He always expected his younger brother, who was not retired like he was, to do these things in addition to the help that he was already providing to them.

I was later told by this same brother that when they had asked him when he would come for a visit, he had claimed that I was too sick to travel, and that we couldn't leave at the time.

I had told his brother, "That's interesting, because I always used to ask him when we were going to go see them."

I had been at the store with one of my only friends when Grandpa called me out of the blue. Concerned that something might be wrong (I usually called him, not the other way around) I answered almost immediately.

"Hi, hun!" boomed his cheery voice on the other end of the line.

Instantly I felt at ease, as I could tell by his greeting that everything was business as usual. If something had been wrong, he wouldn't have answered that way. That was how he always greeted me, with those exact same words, voice inflection and all, with much warmth and excitement.

Grandpa had called me to tell me that he and Grandma were coming for a visit in a few weeks, but not to tell my parents because he wanted to surprise them.

As I reflect back on these events now, I believe that Grandpa had suspected that something was wrong behind closed doors. Not only had Grandpa noticed my obvious obesity, he had also noticed my shyness and lack of self-confidence. He probably noticed a comment that I had once made about how we had to scramble to clean the house anytime company came. It was no wonder, as Mother was a complete hoarder. I think Grandpa wanted an honest glimpse into my living conditions, and I think he suspected that Father wouldn't let anyone else in. Unfortunately, these are things that I didn't come to realize until a handful of years passed on.

A week later, as promised, Grandma and Grandpa arrived. Not surprisingly, the house was a complete mess, therefore Mother and Father were mortified. Especially Mother. But I honored my Grandpa, and had refused to disobey his command, especially since he treated me much, much nicer than Father or Mother did.

Father always says family shouldn't hide things. If that's true and the family will accept relatives the way they are, why is it such a big deal that Grandpa and Grandma are seeing how things really are?

Later, after Grandma and Grandpa left, Father scolded me profusely for not letting him and Mother in on the impending visit. I didn't hear the end of it for a week, yet surprisingly, I didn't get hit for it.

Months later, I called Grandpa just to chat. Casually, during our conversation, he mentioned that if I wanted to, I could come and live with him and Grandma down there.

The idea instantly excited me, but I told Grandpa that I would have to think about it. While I liked the idea, I was extremely unsure of moving, as any kind of change made me extremely uneasy, to say the least.

Sadly, I didn't yet fully realize that my living situation was unusual, or that I was being controlled. Although I realized that things weren't right, I often stuffed my thoughts and emotions down in order to handle the harsh reality I was living with.

I began seriously considering taking Grandpa up on his offer to move in with them, but, as usual, Father had his manipulative tactics at the ready.

He had carefully crafted a speech, saying, "Grandma and Grandpa are just offering to be nice. They want to take care of you, but they're really too old to be dealing with all of that. Mom and I have to constantly care for you, and they don't need to be dealing with all the anxiety attacks and depression. You're bringing us down constantly with your depression. Do you really wanna do that to them? They love ya, but they're too old for that shit."

As if those words weren't convincing enough, he added, "Besides, you wouldn't have any friends there. And you only have *one* here." As if I didn't already feel pathetic enough.

The empathy he so eloquently displayed in his voice along with on his face is nauseating as I look back on it now, realizing in hindsight how expertly I was manipulated and controlled. He really was an excellent faker.

I would later come to realize what an expert Father was at pouring salt into already exposed, deep, gaping wounds. Even worse was that he seemed to gain enjoyment from it. Seeing how far he could push people and how much he could manipulate them seemed to be like a hobby to him. People were merely pawns in his game, with him being the all-powerful chess master.

A while after his passing, Grandma showed me the letters Grandpa had written to her while he had been away in the army. I heard stories about his exploits and bravery in the armed forces, and grew saddened upon realizing that I really hadn't even known him very well at all. I had been so busy being a confused, hateful, angry, teenager that I never even realized that I should have made time with him. And now it was too late. He was gone, and I would never get any more chances to get to know him. That realization made me even angrier at Father. He would've known that I should've made the time with Grandpa, yet he never cared to tell me to do it, the narcissist that he was.

Now I hate Father even more for not letting me know that I should have made time with Grandpa; for knowingly manipulating me into not moving in with him. Not only did that keep me sick, it also deprived me of the chance to really know Grandpa.

I hate the hospital for being negligent while Grandpa was in their care. That resulted in Grandpa's death.

I hate that the last memory I have of Grandpa is him looking sickly before going back to the hospital.

I'm angry at God for allowing Grandpa to be taken from me too soon, and for not letting me see for so many long, agonizing years that Father was manipulating me.

I wonder about the times I could've had with Grandpa. I want to know the stories of his life, all about him. I missed out on all of that. And now the opportunity is gone and I can't get it back. Just like Mother.

I'm ashamed to say that I barely knew the wonderful man. I mean, by all accounts he was wonderful. But so was Father, supposedly. And with that comment, I feel very confused and this is all just too hard to comprehend.

My head hurts now.

As usual, Father and I embarked on our nightly trip to our local ice cream shop. He seemed to enjoy treating me to an extra-large dessert every night, saying, "You deserve it for trying so hard to work."

All of those sugary desserts in combination with my frequent cravings for comfort foods had made me obese, which caused Father to look at me in disgust at my size.

Both parents told me many times that I shouldn't eat so much, which would tell them the cause of my cravings. "Food tastes good, and the experience of taste is the only pleasurable experience I ever have. And that pleasure is the only thing that very slightly reduces the severe pain I'm constantly in."

Besides, Mother had made it a point to let me know frequently that, "I need you!" Compulsive eating was the only way other than suicide to deal with the immense pain of life.

Unfortunately I was still too jaded to realize that Father was the cause of all that pain.

"I'm eating myself half to death for you," I used to tell Mother, "so you won't have the pain of losing me."

After all, I'm nothing and have nothing worth living for, so I'm only existing for everyone else. As horrible as I am, maybe doing the selfless deed of wrecking my health with overeating will negate some of my worthlessness and inferiority in the afterlife...if there is one.

As Father drove us home from the ice cream shop, we started arguing, a result of yet another slew of derogatory comments about me. Arguing was something we did almost constantly, so in this particular instance, I don't recall what even started this argument, or what it was about.

However, his temper rose more than normal this time, evident by the hand that he had raised above my leg. He actually caught himself (a big surprise to me) and froze there for a moment, his hand hovering over me ominously.

After a minute, he lowered that hand slowly. Then, as if he were aware that I was not capable of thinking on my own, he smiled kindly like he did in front of his friends and said, "You know I'd never really hit you."

As most of my memories were still repressed, I didn't consciously remember that he had done so before. Subconsciously, though, part of my brain must have, as evident from the response I gave.

Terrified, and unable to look in Father's direction, something deep within me had snapped as I responded brazenly, "Yeah, because you know I'd beat the shit out of you right back."

Although I wasn't even looking at him, I did observe, out of the corner of my eye, the jolt of shock he displayed, as he stared in my direction, taken aback.

That's when it hit me: *He's just a big bully who never grew up. Underneath his mask, he's still an insecure little kid.*

That's when I subconsciously began to realize what my therapist had meant when she had said that I was allowing him to have power over me.

Age 24

It was the night before Thanksgiving when we received a call from the Robbins. They wanted to know if we had seen Ben, as his fiancé hadn't heard from him. She had gone over to their house to pick him up since they were supposed to go over to her family's house for the holiday. When she didn't find him, she called his mother, in a bit of a panic.

They had already contacted his friends and none of them knew his whereabouts either. The family had grown increasingly worried. This wasn't like him, and we all knew it. He had a troubled past, sure, but he had been on the straight and narrow for years after having done a few stints in juvenile hall.

Father let them know that we hadn't seen him, and promised that if we did, we would let them know.

For the next several hours, I prayed for Ben constantly, completely consumed by worry. Granted I hadn't spent much time with the family for the past handful of years, but the history I had with them still held a special place in my heart. Being next door neighbors who were close in age, I had grown up very closely with all of them. I still thought of them as "my other family."

The truth was that I had missed them all terribly but was too afraid to cause a riff between myself and Father. It was obvious that he didn't think very highly of them. And what could I do about it? I knew that I was unable to work. It would be asinine to cause a riff with the person who controlled my finances. Besides, I was terrified to even consider hanging out with them, especially after his comment about how he thought Cathy should be shot. I felt that causing a riff could also potentially cause my death at the hands of my own father.

Yet, because of all the outsiders who still made comments praising Father, telling me he is "such a great Dad to you, isn't he?" I still did not realize that my situation was unusual or wrong.

Hours passed until the phone rang again, caller ID indicating that it was one of the Robbins'. Father answered, an air of fakeness in his voice as usual.

He hated religion and anything having to do with it, so I knew instantly by his comment that something was seriously wrong.

Before hanging up the phone, he ended the call with, "You guys take care, okay? And God bless."

"Did they find Ben?" I questioned.

The bluntness of Father's response struck me extra harshly, like several knife blades being dragged deep within the flesh of my fingertips.

"They found him dead!" Father announced.

What the fuck...

I didn't even really know what to do with that comment or how to process the horrible reality of the situation.

After a few seconds, Mother questioned, "What happened?"

"They don't know yet," Father proclaimed. "His friend went over to the house looking for him and found him. The police are over there now trying to figure out what happened."

"Oh my goodness!" Mother exclaimed, her surprise evident by the look on her face.

Even still Father kept at it with the derogatory comments, "Honestly my guess is drugs."

Of course you'd say that, you judgmental asshole! Ben probably isn't even cold yet and you can't even be nice for one second! You never hesitate to tear down anyone who was ever associated with me, do you?

I felt sick to my stomach at his heartless comment.

That poor family just lost their son, and all you can do is be fake over the phone and then judge him behind their backs?!

I wanted to say goodbye to my friend, so I began walking out the door and over to their house anyway, ignoring Father's pleas not to go.

For the first time in history, I was so mad that I shouted at him, rather than fearing him as per my usual, "That's my friend and I want to honor him!" I shouted as I walked next door, leaving Father standing in the doorway.

Once I approached the scene, a policeman stopped me and asked if I had known Ben. "Yes," I said.

Then he proceeded to ask me questions about Ben. "How old was he?"

Ben's best friend, who had endured the horror of discovering his cold, lifeless body, overheard the policeman's question.

This friend instantly snapped, "They don't know a God damn thing!" he shouted, pain evident in his voice. "He was my best friend!" The tears rolled down his cheeks.

Instantly I realized that it would be more appropriate for me to let his best friend answer the officer's questions given such a painful and unexpected turn of events. I stepped politely aside in silence, offering my friend's best friend a comforting half smile. That was all that I could muster, although I realized that my smile did nothing to comfort him, and that there was nothing I would ever be able to say or do to make him feel better.

I barely have any friends, and one of them just died. Nice! What else can go wrong in my life?

The rest of the night was spent mourning Ben's loss while I simultaneously tried to make sense of it all.

Why, God, why? Why would you let this happen? You took from me one of my only friends! Aren't I miserable enough?! Don't I suffer enough every day? I've been asking for thirteen years for you to take me home, and you take Ben instead? He wasn't even asking to go home with you. Why? Why would you take him? And why won't you take me?! I'm the one who's miserable. Ben had a family, and a fiancé, he was getting married! Why, God? Why?!! He was happy here! I'm miserable, and have been for so many years! Why?! Why would you choose Ben over me?!!

I was convinced that I was unable to work and that therefore the only way out of that house was to find a guy and get married and have him support me. That was the example led by Mother, so why would I think any differently? It wouldn't be until years later that I would come to realize that she is codependent, and that codependency is a bad thing.

Things once got so bad that I told her I was going to marry any guy willing to take care of me financially just so I could get out of that house. Of course, Father convinced her, as he always did, that I was just exaggerating.

Days later, the psychiatrist asked me to admit to her the same thing, that I had been exaggerating. So, I did...but only to spare mom's feelings, even though I really had meant it, and was desperately looking for someone willing to help me so that I could actually do it.

Later on, I attempted yet another time to get people to start asking questions.

If I can get anyone to question things, I will finally be able to get away, because then people will start realizing what I've been saying is true and that my living situation isn't safe.

A neighbor had messaged me via text to ask how I was doing. It was no secret that I was struggling with crippling anxiety and depression, and I figured that eventually people would realize that my living situation was the cause of that. I responded to her message, saying that I was "hanging in there" and "trying to take it day by day."

She responded with, "I'm glad you're having an ok day. You're lucky to have parents that care so much."

This is my window of opportunity! An empathic person who holds so much stock in doing what's right will believe me. She will know it's against God to assume anything, and God wouldn't let anyone else not take me seriously, especially after all these years of suffering. He knows I need help. And I mean, I've even been to church with these people. Father is really going to be sorry he abused me now!

Bluntly telling people that my father was abusive and berated me surely wouldn't work, as he was such an expert at convincing people about anything. I figured that if I was more mature about it, and didn't give specifics, it would sound less like an accusation and more like what it really was: a plea for help.

Taking the bull by the horns, I utilized my window of opportunity, responding, "Behind closed doors, my parents actually aren't that nice to me."

I was hoping that she had gotten busy, as she didn't respond for the rest of that day. Over time, however, I began to realize that she must have not believed me, or she didn't want to be "in the middle of things" as the expression goes, as that ended up being the last time I ever heard from her.

Why is God allowing me to be in this abusive situation? Maybe I'm not doing something right. Maybe He wants me to start going to church. And if I start going to church, Mother will start taking me seriously when I tell her Father shouldn't abuse us. I mean, she says she can't divorce him because it's a sin. If I find religious people who say it's not a sin, then she'll finally leave him, and I can have my mom back! Afterall, God's promise says He will heal her and she will be my mom again!

Sadly, this beyond adolescent age of twenty-four was the time in life when I finally decided to obtain my driver's license. I enjoyed my new-found freedom gained by earning it. Father decided to purchase a new car, during which time I asked him, "what are you going to do with the old one?"

Believing that I was worthless and inferior, I was shocked to hear him say that he was going to give the car to me.

What a nice Dad I have! Only a great man would give his old car to his useless, inadequate daughter who isn't even capable of working. I don't deserve the car, or his kindness. Maybe I have been too hard on him. Maybe everyone is right, he really is a great guy. What other kind of person would give a car to someone this inferior? Maybe everyone's right, and the abuse is all in my head.

The Awakening

A ge 25

Feeling miserable and alone, I started searching for church groups to go to. I went online and discovered one that was for singles, so I added it to my busy, unemployed schedule. It fit perfectly between my listening to music and my pre recorded television viewing before bed.

I had been looking for the singles group of people my age. My main mission was to find companionship. At this point, my relationship with God was actually a forced attempt at attaining some sliver of hope, so I didn't care about the religious aspect of the group. Although that aspect was quite appealing to me... I figured that religious people were loyal to a fault, like Mother.

Going to a religious group is exactly what I need because it is a sin if they don't "love thy brethren." So they will have to like me. Or at the very least, they won't abandon me like the family, friends, and neighbors who don't believe me have. Or avoid me like Father, who always tells me that my depression is "too much."

As it turns out, I ended up going into the wrong group, but didn't find out until the evening was almost over that I was in the wrong place. Instead of going to the room with the singles group that was my age, which was further down the hall, I ended up in the room with the singles that were closer to my parents' age. I enjoyed myself more than I probably would have if I had gone to the other group. I have always been an old soul in a young body, gravitating towards people older than myself.

I started attending regularly, and because of these newfound friends of mine, I started coming back into the faith. I started attending church more, participating in a few other groups as well. One of these groups was a young adult group where I met a lot of new people and started actually developing a social life.

However, the worse my depression got, the more I felt like a few of these so-called friends were avoiding me. One of these supposed "friends" would later go on to tell someone behind my back that I was "too much for her," and that "I guess I'm just a horrible person" for refusing to help me during a time of need.

Later, one of these women and I grew quite close, and spent most of our days together. She had severe physical limitations, I enjoyed helping her clothe herself and feed herself, and even enjoyed helping her use the toilet, as the fact that she was unable to do these things for herself gave me a sense of purpose. For once in my life, I felt like something other than a burden. This woman made me feel valuable and wanted, which were things I never thought I would ever be capable of being. She referred to me as her "best friend," and would say that we were going to be in each other's lives forever; that we would grow old together. I took her to concerts despite the fact that I never cared for her preferred music genre. As a matter of fact, it was well known to anyone who knew me that I couldn't stand that Country music. It was not just the style of it or those stereotypical twangy, whiny sounds, but every Country song seems to be about the same two things. First the couple romances, then later the woman takes off in the singer's recently fixed broken down truck and leaves him heartbroken.

I had come to the conclusion that a person with another disability was safe and would not abandon me.

She has a disability and several struggles of her own, so she wouldn't ignore my struggles like everybody else does just because they aren't visible...Right??

But, yet again, when my depression grew increasingly bad, she accused me of "wanting attention" and told me to "focus on my family and friends, then you won't be depressed."

What family? The family that makes me feel like a piece of shit? And what friends? What you're saying right now makes me feel like I really don't have any friends. It's clear that no one even remotely understands me. You're just like everyone else: none of you even know me at all.

I understood that because of her condition, she was not capable of really comprehending what I was going through, but that didn't stop her words and lack of empathy from cutting me deeply. The real kick in the head, however, was that, while we were out, strangers would often purchase meals for her because of her obvious disability. But she had a job. I wasn't able to work and even had a service dog, but people always assumed that it was hers.

Everyone can see her disability but because mine aren't visible, people assume that mine must be all in my head. People buy her meals but she's able to hold down a job. I'll just continue to watch people buy meals for someone who can actually work. Guess I'll just keep going broke. Guess no one will ever see me. Even with this friend who has a disability, I am beginning to be invisible. No one will ever care about me or what happens to me. No one will ever see my value.

I couldn't believe that I had been thrown away yet again, this time by someone who couldn't even care for themselves. She seemed completely oblivious to the myriad of things that I had done for her. She was another person who vowed that they would always be there for me, and, in the end, lied, stabbed me through the heart, and discarded me like I was never anything at all.

Wow. Discarded again, like a piece of trash. I'm so pathetic that even a person who can't take care of themselves doesn't want me. Here's proof that I'm worthless. I guess I really am trash. Why do Father and Mother put up with me?

Depression is wild. Your brain will always look for evidence that the story it's feeding you is the truth. And I had plenty of evidence coming my way. After that, I realized that the only person worth keeping in my life was my real best friend, the person who had been in my life for several years, Rose.

Rose and I had met several years prior, back in elementary school, during a pageant the school was putting on. Years later, she admitted to me that she had seen me and instantly thought I was really cool, although she couldn't give a reason why. Rose was one of the most kind-hearted people one will ever meet, one of the few truly good people in the world who possesses few flaws. She always greets people with a smile, and never has a bad thing to say about anyone. She is completely non-judgmental, and goes above and beyond to lift people up with compliments. Secretly, I wondered why she put up with me, and honestly thought it was because she felt sorry for me. That was the main reason I was afraid to go to her during times of need. I was afraid that if I did, she would abandon me too.

During another fight with Mother regarding Father, she criticized me again after I had mentioned that I could not stand him and that I found him repulsive and repugnant in every way. I then broached the subject of some of Father's nasty habits, asking her if she had really not noticed that he never really washed his hands after using the bathroom, but only pretended to, or the putrid anal smell on Father's recliner, or the fact that he had a habit of picking his nose.

"He doesn't do any of those things," she responded shortly.

Wow. Bad enough that their friends accuse me of making things up, now even Mother, my hero, is doing it! Seriously, does anyone know me at all?! She always says that she knows that I wouldn't lie or make things up, yet she still accuses me of doing it? I seem shocked by it but I know why. Because she refuses to believe or acknowledge any of his flaws. She's placed him too high up on a pedestal.

Her accusation made me hate Father even more, especially as I watched him digging for gold again during a TV show, then proceeded to roll the mucus around on his fingers before flinging it across the room, where it landed noticeably on the white wall. Gosh he was disgusting. Later, upon investigation, I was mortified to find several boogers on that particular wall, thus causing me to forever refer to that wall as "the booger wall."

Eventually, Mother confessed, "You're right, Eliza. He doesn't really wash his hands. He turned the water on, ran his fingers under it, dried them, then turned off the water."

"I told you!" I exclaimed. "He's gross!"

"They say love is blind," responded Mother.

Later that evening, in casual conversation, she looks at me and says, "You're right, his chair does have a nasty smell."

Again, I responded with, "I told you! He's disgusting!"

And again, Mother responded with, "Love is blind."

She would often respond with those same three horrifying words after I had asked her how she could stay with someone who treated me so badly.

I used to enjoy sleeping in the basement. It felt like having my own little apartment. It was a way for me to mentally escape the reality of the hell I was living in. One day, Father had to call some repairmen out to the house to fix the sump pump, and he said they would be there "sometime tomorrow."

That night, I went to sleep on the couch in the basement, as usual. In the morning, however, I was awakened by the sound of unknown male voices. Startled and uneasy, I slowly raised up and peered over the back of the couch to find a team of three repairmen walking down the basement stairs, led by Father!

What the hell! He knows I sleep in my underwear, and he's letting strange men, three of them, into the area where his teenage daughter is sleeping?!!

Appalled, I hid under the covers until the men had gone into the back room of the basement so I knew I would be out of their view. Angry as a hornet, I grabbed my clothes and quickly dressed myself, my heart and mind racing, the whole time chanting, "Please don't come back out, please don't come back out, please don't come back out."

Luckily, my half nakedness went undiscovered by any of the men. After they left, I proceeded to grill Father about his complete lack of empathy.

"Why didn't you wake me?!" I questioned, still appalled at my supposed caretaker's actions.

"I tried," he responded unempathetically, "You didn't hear me."

Seriously?!! You barely even tried! What if these men have criminal records? What if they had discovered me while still asleep and tried to take advantage of me? Would you have even defended me? Or would you even have noticed if they had tried? Or would you have even cared if they did? Clearly, Father doesn't value me in the least.

Realizing that Father did not care at all about the danger he could've put me in, much less my feelings, I decided to drop the subject, and that I would later take it up with Mother when she got home.

Hours later, when she arrived, I told her what had happened. She displayed an annoyed look, as if she knew I had been embarrassed to have almost been seen in my underwear. Seemingly oblivious to the danger he could've put me in, she stated simply, "Well that wasn't very nice of him."

Wow. I'm living with two children. He doesn't want to be bothered and she is completely naïve.

"Mom!" I urged. "You need to have a talk with him!"

"Your father has his own way of doing things," she responded. "I'm sure he realizes his actions weren't cool."

What...the...fuck.

Beyond frustrated, I continued, "Those men could've tried to hurt me. We don't know them! They could have criminal records for all we know!"

Why do I even have to explain this?!! And why isn't a supposed adult able to think of this on their own?!!

"I didn't even think of that!" she exclaimed nervously, finally grasping the severity of the situation.

"Yeah!" I rolled my eyes openly, not minding at all whether or not she was offended, and knowing that she most definitely was.

"So..." I prodded, waiting for Mother to realize that she needed to do something about the situation.

"So, what?" Mother said.

Again, I rolled my eyes, intentionally more rudely this time. "So you'll talk to him?"

"Yeah, I'll talk to him." Mother responded in a low tone, as if she was not looking forward to talking with him.

I could detect the lack of confidence in her voice.

Later Father confronted me about this conversation and several others that Mother had had with him after my prompting. He grumbled angrily at me, calling me a "tattle tale" under his breath.

When I later recounted this comment to Mother, she responded insecurely with, "What am I, his mother?!"

Years later, when the subject arose again, Mother and I began arguing about it. I asked her why she had allowed Father to put me through so many unsafe situations, telling her how scared I had been.

Her response was, "You never told me you were scared."

I didn't realize I had to. I thought you were supposed to have maternal instinct. And this isn't even maternal instinct, this is common sense!

At the beginning of the singles church group one night, I had shared that I was glad I was there instead of home, as Father and I had been in yet another argument. I told them that he had become angry that I refused to give specifics about text messages he'd seen on my phone. He had angrily asked "Who is this Bill guy?" I had also shared with them that I had been late because I had to pull over to reset my phone since Father had called to tell me that I had to. He couldn't see me on the tracker.

After the conclusion of the meeting, one of my newfound friends, Heather, asked if she could speak to me alone for a minute. I wondered what it was she wanted to talk about but I followed her to the corner of the room anyway. She appeared slightly uneasy.

"What do you mean your dad couldn't see you on the tracker?" Heather questioned.

I tilted my head to one side, realizing the expression of concern on her face. The fact that she was asking me about it and the fact that she had called me into a separate corner suddenly made me wonder if, just maybe, that situation wasn't normal.

After a long pause, I asked her, "Is that not normal?"

She responded, "No. Not at your age."

Then I wondered if maybe some of the other things Father did were abnormal.

Finally putting two and two together, I asked, "What about entering my passcode and reading my messages and scrolling through photos?"

Heather paused, seemingly noting the realization that must've been showing on my face.

"Is that not supposed to happen?" I asked, almost desperately, wondering if it was possible that I had been wronged and duped by Father all those years of my life.

My face must have revealed my shock and awe, as my friend lowered her voice empathetically, responding comfortingly, "No, honey. That's not supposed to happen."

Then she hugged me and told me that if I ever needed to talk, I could always call her.

Lying in bed that night, I finally began questioning everything about Father and my previous feeling about him abusing me returned. Only this time I no longer suspected in the back of my mind that any of it was in my head. I was learning not to question my reality any longer. I finally realized there was a problem. I had no idea what to do about it and wondered, even if there was, would I be *able* to do anything about it?

At least someone finally cares enough about me to give me the benefit of the doubt. Finally, after all these long, torturous years. I knew from then on I could call Heather for any questions I had regarding him. I knew that she would tell me the truth.

Unfortunately for Heather, she would later learn that I literally could not think on my own. I had spent so many years being told what to think and do and how to do it. I no longer had any idea of what was real and what wasn't. She quickly learned that I would need her help with every possible decision I would ever make. She knew that no one else had ever helped me and realized that it was very possible that, if she didn't, no one else would.

My depression was to the point that it was severely afflicting me on a daily basis. I had at least one breakdown a day, usually more. Mother was always there for me. I would call her whenever I became suicidal. I would let her know I wasn't safe and then she would come sit upstairs in my room with me. Father couldn't stand these constant interruptions. He would have to pause the television show he was watching so that Mother wouldn't miss it. I could tell that he hated me for that but I also realized that he wasn't doing anything to help me. Instead, he chose to berate me, saying, "God damn it, Eliza!" Don't start *that* shit again!"

It was no wonder my days were plagued with constant anxiety attacks. On some level I realized that I wasn't even allowed to process my emotions in my own home. Eventually I began needing to go to the ER quite often because the anxiety affected me so badly that my throat would start constricting until I could barely breathe. Riddled with panic and fear as to whether or not I would be able to continue to breathe, I always drove myself there because Mother never took my anxiety seriously. Father had long ago convinced her it was all in my head.

Almost every week, Father would have a talk with me when Mother was out shopping. "You shouldn't tell people when you're depressed. You should keep it to yourself because you're bringing everybody else down." I couldn't believe he asked me to push down my depression. To which I would reply, "I'm not trying to." And would proceed to continue to pretend that nothing was wrong and I was ok.

While I realized that what Father said was true, I was telling people how depressed I was as a cry for help. I was hoping people would finally realize that my living situation was the problem and that Father was nothing but an excellent faker. I used to put pleas for help on social media, posting comments like, "Well, here I am again, driving myself to the ER because no one cares," and "I hope I don't die tonight," hinting at my suicidal thoughts. All the while I was hoping and praying that someone, anyone would sense my desperation and figure out that things weren't right and actually care enough to help get me out of that house. Unfortunately no one ever called me after those posts. No one ever came to my rescue. They probably thought I was just being dramatic. Just like my parents did.

Father quickly grew fed up with all of that, telling me often, "We had a lot more fun before you came along. Then once you came along, we couldn't have any fun anymore."

Then if you hate me so much, just kill me off. I hate my life anyway. There is nothing worth living for, and because of you, I barely have any quality of life. And because of you, everyone hates me and won't take me seriously. You try living with this agony and see how you like it, asshole!

My pulmonologist later informed Mother and I that my lungs were severely inflamed, and my lungs were only functioning at 40%. The doctor informed us that the problem could not be my anxiety, and that it must be something in the house that I was allergic to, which was why my throat would close up until I got to the ER. Father convinced Mother that I was allergic to the cats, which were both hypoallergenic. I knew better. The house always smelled musty, but of course, Mother believed Father, who had also convinced everyone else of that too.

Father had always insinuated to others that my depression was biologically hereditary, passed down to me by the mother that gave birth to me. And he really loved the reaction he gained from others when they came to the conclusion that my seemingly innocent, loving parents were taking great care of me despite the problems passed down to all of us from my biological relatives.

I could hear family friends saying things like, "Those poor parents, having to care for Eliza with her severe mental illness that she inherited." "Paul is such a good person for helping her, despite how exhausting it must be for him to have to care for both of them so often."

Because I believed it too, I used to feel so bad for Mother and Father.

Those poor people couldn't have kids of their own and then got stuck with my dysfunctional ass. I can't do anything right and can't even take care of myself. Hell, I can't even breathe correctly, and they're stuck putting up with it. I know they don't want to, but feel obligated to help me, because they know no one else would. What great parents I have! I feel so sorry for everyone who has the burden of having me in their life. I just wish I could function or at least take care of myself. Or that everyone would finally just let me die.

In an attempt to acquire the help I needed, therapy was always a part of my life. As severe as my depression was, I saw a total of five therapists throughout the first twenty-five years of my life and would go on to see even more later on.

The first four therapists had told me that if Father hadn't been the one to raise me, I wouldn't have depression or anxiety or have so much trouble functioning. However, because my living situation was so painful and I had no way out without being able to hold down a job, my brain chose to hide that information from me in order to cope in that horrible environment. It wasn't until after I finally escaped that I remembered those comments.

The fifth therapist, whom I saw longer than any of the others, said this as well, yet she reminded me often, knowing that I needed to know that in order to be able to get out of that broken home. After having heard it several more times, I then remembered that the other therapists had said it too.

This is it! Mother always puts so much stock in religion, and since the therapist is with God and goes to church, Mother will listen once I tell her that it's been proven by five separate therapists that Father really is the problem. Now Mother will finally see Father for what he really is, and she'll do the right thing and take me out of there so I can heal and begin to function!

During another argument with Mother about Father, I asked her, "You trust the therapist, right?"

"Yes I do," she replied.

"Well, I keep telling you he's the problem and you won't listen to me," I stated. "Five out of five therapists that I've now seen even said that if it weren't for him, I wouldn't have depression, anxiety, or not be able to function!"

"They shouldn't have said that!" she responded defensively.

What the hell is wrong with you?!! Still?!! Seriously?!! You're offended because people said something against your beloved husband?! So the therapists shouldn't tell me the facts needed in order for me to be okay and hopefully heal one day?!!

I didn't know what else to say to that and was beginning to wonder if there was even anything else I could say that would make Mother ever take me seriously or consider my feelings for once.

Age 26

At this point, the psychological abuse and gaslighting continued to grow worse as time went on. I could tell by his insults and curses that Father came to hate me more and more. I could tell that he was ashamed of me more than ever now. He would constantly criticize my overeating and would refer to me as a "fat slob."

He once even looked at me, his face exhibiting complete disgust and said, "You used to be such a knockout and, well, look at you now."

I reminded both he and Mother that I had to overeat in order to deal with the immense pain of existence, which Father found as an excuse as well as yet another thing to use to discredit me, telling more people, "She suffers from some severe depression, anxiety issues, and some autism."

During another nightly argument between Mother and I about Father, as usual, even she began criticizing my eating habits. Again, I reminded her that I was only doing it for her, because she said she needed me, and the only other way to deal with that pain was suicide.

During these arguments, she would often say, "When people have kids, they usually move out by now!"

To which I would always respond, "Like I keep telling you, I can't move out! You don't seem to understand that right now, you're only getting fifty percent of the abuse. If I was to move out, you would get all of it, one hundred percent of the abuse. I love you and can't do that to you! I can't leave you alone with that monster!"

Eventually she will see that he's abusing her, after all, everyone from church keeps reminding me of God's promise and that His promise says there will be healing and she can be okay again. Sacrificing myself for my only real family member will be worth it later once she is finally free from his abuse.

One night, after yelling at Mother for several minutes that I could not take being around Father one more second or else I would kill myself, Mother called her friend who was out of town to vent. Her friend then offered to let Mother and I stay at their house while she and her family were away so that I could get the distance I needed. While there, Mother ended up calling their son, who works in the medical field, to get his advice on what he thought should be done about me. After the phone call, Mother entered the room where I was and said, "He thinks you should go to the stress center if the feeling of being suicidal persists."

"I've been there once already and it only made things worse," I respond- ed. "Besides, how will that help long term when the problem is Father?

Unless I can get away from him, things will never change for me." Mother ignored my comment.

It was painful hearing from her friend's son that he thought I should go to the stress center. It was clear from the fact that he barely communicated with me anymore that he, just like several other people who used to be a regular part of my life, no longer wanted anything to do with me.

Here's another person I thought would never leave me now avoids me like the plague since my depression got bad. We practically grew up together. When we were kids, his mom used to tell my mom that he missed me and then our parents would get together so we could see each other. What happened to that relationship? Why did he stop being close to me once depression set in? We used to be like siblings, and now we're basically estranged, all because he can't handle my depression? I can't either but the only way I can leave it behind is to take my own life. Why doesn't anyone understand this?! Why do I have to suffer alone? Why doesn't anyone care?

Years later, I would come to see the irony of the whole situation. The fact that I improved slightly once Father wasn't around should have been an indicator to people, especially after having tried to tell them that there were family problems. Yet somehow no one that knew the family ever put two and two together.

My depression was making it more and more difficult for me to show up for work most of the time. After several failed attempts at holding down a job, Father and I applied for social security disability income.

Finally! It's about time they take me seriously. I've only been telling them for years that it's not that I don't want to work, but that I can't. Now, once I get the income from disability, I will finally be able to sever ties from Father and won't need to live off of him anymore. Then Mother will see how much healthier I am, and stop living in denial, and she will leave too. And then I will get my mom back and then she and I can have our own safe, healthy family.

Again I find myself and Mother in the midst of yet another heated argument about Father's abuse.

"I don't understand why you stay with someone who makes us suffer so much!" I shouted.

"He is my husband!" Mother shouted back, like always.

"I know. 'You can't get a divorce because it's a sin,'" I mocked. "I told you, he's not married to you. He's selfish and married to himself, which as per my church group, gives you the right to divorce him, sin free."

"He doesn't mean it," was the excuse she so often offered.

"If he didn't mean it, he wouldn't keep doing it," I responded.

Realizing that Father was using religion to manipulate her, I didn't ever want to resort to manipulation. I never wanted to do anything like Father. I saw an opportunity for manipulation and didn't want to use it but I had been trying everything else for several years to no avail. Knowing she held so much stock in religion and lived in constant fear of doing anything against God, I said, "Which do you think God would find to be a worse sin: divorcing your abusive husband, or allowing your innocent daughter to suffer at his hands from a young age until she hated her miserable life so much that death would be better for her?"

It was evident by her lack of response and blank stare that Mother was in deep thought over that comment.

After waiting a minute, I decided to leave Mother alone in the room to think about that. I then went to my own room and prayed. It was clear that I had finally, after all those years, struck a nerve with Mother, a breakthrough which I thanked God for. I also asked God, yet again, to bring the light to Mother so that she would see the truth and leave him and stop suffering in the mind of her abusive husband who claimed to love her.

The next night, another argument ensued, as if it were scheduled.

Again, I asked her the same question I had asked her the previous night, "Which do you think God would find to be a worse sin: divorcing your abusive husband, or allowing your innocent daughter to suffer at his hands from a young age until death was the best option for her?"

She immediately looked disappointed, responding in a lowered tone, "We can't move out. I don't make enough money to support you on my own."

I was shocked, saying, "You can't get a job temporarily until I can work?!"

She had nothing to say, but her lack of confidence was evident on her face. She was scowling, disappointedly.

It was then I realized that the only way she could've come to that conclusion was if Father had specifically gone out of his way to tell her that. He had, yet again, manipulated her into allowing both of us to endure abuse. That was the day I realized that Father was Mother's confidant, that she went to him with everything I would ever say to her, therefore, nothing I would ever say to her would stay between the two of us.

Nothing is sacred anymore.

Because I rarely connected with people my own age, it was typical for me to venture back to some of my schools and visit my former teachers. During one visit with a former high school teacher, I decided to tell her about how abusive Father was. She empathized with me and asked, "Is he an alcoholic?" I explained to her that he never touched the stuff, so no. However, I would later learn that the term "dry drunk" perfectly described him with his rage and snap judgments of others. Although I could tell that the situation was something that my former teacher wasn't exactly sure how to handle, she provided me with the name of a local organization that specifically helped victims of crime as well as abusive situations.

I looked up information about the place she had suggested and even went so far as to travel there in person. Security was top notch, which made me feel nervous upon entering. No one could simply walk through the front door. Instead, I had to ring the doorbell to gain access.

Upon pushing the button, a female voice questioned, "Yes?"

Not having expected that situation and unsure of exactly how to respond, I answered the unknown voice in a quiet, shy tone, "I'm in an abusive situation."

"Come on in," the warm voice answered as the light on the keypad on the locked door turned from red to green.

I opened the door, walked in, and looked around to find a waiting room and a receptionist, obviously the source of the formerly unknown voice.

"Hi," she greeted me with a smile, "How are you?"

I offered my usual response, "I'm hanging in there."

"We just need you to fill out these forms, and then someone will be right with you," she stated, holding up the paperwork on a clipboard and offering me a pen.

I grabbed the items and sat down. It asked for name, date of birth, address, the typical things...and then it asked why I was there.

My heart felt as if it would pound out of my chest as I wrote down: In an abusive living situation.

Then my heart dropped at the next line: Name of abuser:

My heart raced even faster, although I had previously thought that wasn't possible, and my cheeks flushed with redness that seemed to burn my face.

Suddenly, I felt as if the walls were closing in on me, and panic ensued.

I can't do this. He tracks me on my phone and uses my passcode to look at my texts and photos. There's no way he wouldn't figure out I'm here a lot. Hell, he probably already knows I'm here now and that I'm on to his manipulation. I'll get in so much trouble when I get home! Hopefully he doesn't shoot me!

More terrified than ever before, I stood up, set the clipboard and pen on the seat, and bolted out the door.

When I got back home, I was so relieved after several long, nerve-wracking minutes that Father had nothing to say to me. It was clear that he had no idea where I had been or that I had almost defied him.

I'm safe for now.

Weeks passed, and Father had, yet again, pushed me too far. This time was different, though. Something deep within me was completely and utterly fed up. I really couldn't take any more. I hadn't written in my journal in quite a while but was so angry that I decided to write down my feelings after this experience, mainly because I knew how I had a bad habit of making excuses for him later. I finally realized that, unless I wrote these feelings down, preserving them for me to look back on later, I would ultimately keep denying that there was a real problem, like I always had before. I still have the journal entry from that night, Wednesday November 19, 2014. I kept it on my phone, titled, Abusive Father.

"I am so hurt right now. My so-called "Dad" had been continually growing on my nerves today, ever since I rode with him to a few stores. He's almost always cranky these days--about 90 percent of the time. He's so stupid that he doesn't realize it.

One would think that I'd be used to his abuse by now, as it first began at a very young age, and has been growing increasingly worse ever since.

Back to today: I was finally beginning to think that confronting the bastard known as "Dad" would make things better, but instead, it made things worse. He had accused me, as usual, of saying the same thing over and over again. (What am I supposed to do when no one listens to me?)

It was then that I at last decided that maybe he should know the things about himself that I can't stand. I was thinking that maybe he would try to improve himself. I told him many of the things he often does make me feel defeated. I was afraid to look at him when I spoke. I shared with him a feeling I always have because of his plethora of insulting comments towards me.

I said, "Nothing I ever do is good enough for you."

His arrogant reply, which stung me to the core, was, "What do ya want, a medal?"

That was the first time I had ever shared my feelings with him as to how I feel about him. Now I know I'll never make that mistake again. I also wish, for the billionth time, that I could disown my so-called "Dad" without leaving my wonderful mom.

After "Dad" made those harsh and hurtful comments, he continued saying mean and hurtful things about me, but I was too numb with emotional pain at that moment to focus on anything he was saying. My mom, who was in the room witnessing the whole conversation, had to interrupt the mean bastard and tell him not to say anything else to me. She knows how fragile I am and must've been imagining how much that bastard's words hurt me.

He brings out the worst in me. When I'm around him, I snap at people easily (no doubt a result of having heard so much snapping coming from him), I hate life and everything else for that matter, I hate myself for acting like him, I'm very unhappy, I'm angry, and I've lost any ambition and all will to live.

I have to figure out a way to never see him again. Being around him makes everything so much worse. I don't know how much longer I can take this shit! I'm to the point where I've had it. I feel like I almost can't take it anymore and I'm afraid I might snap and lose my temper. I don't want to lash out anymore."

Until just now, I had forgotten that I had even written all of that down. Looking back now, I see the immaturity and lack of complete understanding (at my situation) that I once possessed.

Although the journal entry didn't go into much detail, I remember clearly how Mother reacted to that event.

All I could do was look down at the floor, completely obliterated emotionally as Father continued to insult me after telling him that nothing I ever did was good enough. I deliberately chose not to listen. I knew that Father was livid and never had anything positive to say. The way he continued berating me, it was as if it was his every intention to strip away any remaining dignity or self-love I had left. It seemed like it was his goal to imprison me with insults so that I would never have enough dignity to ever attempt to defy him in any way.

In the midst of his slew of constant insults, Mother could tell how much his attacks were injuring me. For the first time I can remember since age three, she actually defended me against him. I was surprised, because she was always just as afraid as I was to speak out or do anything to go against him. Always the obedient, good little wifey, she never raised her voice or gave him any push back with anything.

For a split second, our mother-daughter connection remained intact as she stood up for me for once. Not only did she interrupt him mid-insult, one better, she actually yelled at him for once!

"Paul!" she shouted in the middle of his sentence.

But he continued nonetheless.

Her voice escalating, she commanded, "Enough! Paul, stop! Just stop! Don't you say anything more to her! Just stop!"

Quite surprised by Mother's sudden burst of strength at standing up to him, I received a second surprise when he actually listened to her, and turned to walk away.

When I knew he was finally gone and out of ear shot, the waterworks started. The tears streamed down my face as I sobbed uncontrollably in front of Mother. She held me in her arms, and for the first time in many years, her hug, and her, all of her, felt completely safe. In fact, at that very moment, Mother felt like home to me for the first time in over twenty years.

That moment didn't last for long. I said, "I don't know how you stand him."

She responded with, "El-i-za! That is your daddy and he loves you!"

As if that precious moment had never happened, the sacred bond between mother and daughter was broken again in an instant. The worst part was that Mother seemed completely oblivious to it all.

After that day, I began distancing myself from Mother even more, absolutely fed up with her constant excuses for him. *What's so special about him? Why does he get to be on a pedestal? Aren't I special to Mother? I guess I'm not enough for her.*

That instance of Father purposefully tearing me down and Mother's continued excuses was what pushed me to my limit. That was what made me say, "I'm done!" At that point, I stopped caring what anyone thought. I no longer cared who would hate me for severing ties with them, or how many people Father would undoubtedly turn against me. I vowed that I would do whatever it took to get away from him.

Even if I have to put his name on the paperwork at the abuse center. It serves him right if people find out what he really is.

The next day, I went back to the abuse center and filled out the paperwork in full, happily listing Father's name as the abuser on the intake form.

Later that week, Mother was bed ridden. She was recovering from a surgical procedure she had to have done. She had been prescribed two pills; a pain pill and an antibiotic, which was standard procedure.

Father prided himself about telling all of their friends that he would be unavailable for the next several weeks as he took care of Mother while she healed. Of course behind closed doors, he complained to me about how he didn't get to do anything he wanted to do for those two weeks because he was "always at her beck and call."

Father went to Mother during the afternoon, surprised that he hadn't heard anything from her in quite a while. He nudged her, saying her name, and she didn't respond. He checked that she was still breathing, then went back into the kitchen where her pills were. Something wasn't sitting right with him. Somehow, Father had given Mother a double dose of the pain medication instead of a dose of each medication.

Upon realizing this, he called the pharmacist, concerned. He explained that he had given her a double dose of the pain medication.

The pharmacist paused, then exclaimed, "She's still alive?!"

"Yes, she's still breathing," Father responded.

I don't remember much after that. I was so concerned about Mother and livid with Father for being so careless.

I avoided him for the rest of the day, all while trying to process the near death of my beloved Mother.

Heather had also been in a previous relationship with someone similar to Father in the past, which is why she had believed me about the abuse, despite the fact that Father was a great actor. When I recounted this event to her, she joined me in wondering whether or not Father's actions may have been intentional, or at least subconsciously so.

"He always complains about taking care of her," I told her, "so it would almost make sense."

"Yeah," Heather nodded as we both considered the possibility.

"I just don't know if he would really do that," I stated. "Maybe on a subconscious level?"

Realizing that Father didn't really care about me as long as I wasn't around to be a bother, I started meeting with advocates at the abuse center on a regular basis. Although I knew he still had access to my location at all times, I figured that as long as I told him I was going there for therapy, he wouldn't question anything. I was right. I would've felt bad lying to him if he had shown any remorse for lying to everyone else constantly but he didn't, so I felt completely comfortable lying to that comfortable liar.

In one of my many sessions with my therapist, I discussed with her the most recent argument between Mother and I, during which I implored her to realize that he is void of empathy and therefore is incapable of loving her, contrary to his claims.

"Why do you say he doesn't have any empathy?" the therapist questioned.

I reminded her of the lies he frequently told his supposed friends, the constant manipulation regardless of how much it hurts others, and recounted two repressed memories: the time he had me threaten the newspaper woman and the incident where I had thrown the toothpaste tube at Mother.

Recognizing this as a red flag, my therapist tried, as she had before, to have the whole family come in together for a session.

Mother was all for it and had attended several sessions with me previously.

Father, on the other hand, always had negative opinions (what else was new) about therapists. Whenever something about him had been brought up in therapy, Mother and I would share the therapist's opinions of him once we arrived back home. He would respond to the therapists' comment, saying, "She doesn't know what she's talking about."

Then why are you sending me? Hypocrite!

As suspected, with much more prodding over the next several months by the therapist, Mother, and myself, Father still refused to join us in a session.

Having matured quite a bit over the past year, I now realized that he was refusing to go because he was scared. I believe that he was afraid of discussing his childhood, which he obviously never learned to deal with. I also believe that, on some level, he was well aware that his behavior was far from normal and suspected what the therapist and I already knew: that he had severe problems of his own, most likely indicative of an undiagnosed illness.

The only excitement I was allotted in life was to go out to lunch or dinner with my best friend, Rose. It was the only time I ever felt at all like I had any kind of a life. It was the only socialization I ever got, other than seeing my therapist and psychiatrist. It was also one of the only opportunities to get out of that house and away from my parents. Any time away from them was a welcome respite from my sad, pathetic existence, and being with Rose was the only real escape I had.

Rose was the sweetest, most genuine person I had ever met, and kind to a fault. She was a dose of how people should treat you...my only dose, unfortunately. Unlike family and supposed friends of the family, she never questioned anything I said or treated me as if I were incapable of taking care of myself. Also different from anyone else in my life was the fact that she was never afraid to answer my phone calls anytime I needed to talk. No matter how depressed or unhappy I was, she would always listen. Even though she didn't always know what to say or how to help me, she never avoided me like others did.

Honestly, I feel guilty because I never realized until later what an integral part Rose played in regard to my survival of all the hardships I endured. Most people can only dream of having a friend as loyal and amazing as Rose. On some level, I always knew this, which is why I never used to discuss many of the traumatic memories I would eventually remember with her. Subconsciously, I feared that even she would leave me.

Why would anyone in their right mind stay with me?

My afternoon or evening meals with Rose were the only normality in my life, and the only guaranteed escape from my parents, albeit temporary. It was the one positive thing in my life that I could count on...until it wasn't.

After arriving home from one of those lunches with Rose, Father summoned me into his office, saying that he needed to talk to me.

"Eliza," he began, "I know you like going out with your friend for lunches and dinners, but unfortunately, with the cost of everything, we can't afford for you to do that anymore." He paused, observing the apparent disappointment on my face, then continued, "I'm sorry. It's just that your medication is so expensive and we're having to pay an arm and a leg for insurance just so you can have it."

At the time, I understood. I would later find out that Father wasn't being truthful.

Of course Father would put an end to that, too. He doesn't want me to have any enjoyment in life.

Age 27

Father's nightly berating followed by my crying to Mother, who offered constant excuses for him never ceased to be a part of the family's evening ritual. Having continued on for several years, I had finally had enough to the point where I had started to realize that my therapist was right. She had told me that Mother would never leave him and warned me that I needed to distance myself in order to ever be okay. The most helpful thing she was telling me was in reference to my expectations that Mother would eventually realize that Father was abusive. She used to tell me, "Insanity is doing the same thing over and over again, expecting a different result."

Fed up with the nightly torture, I decided it was time for me to go. I had informed Father that I was going to leave. I was done living with him. Obviously, with no job and therefore no money, I told him I would move to a homeless shelter until I could get on my feet. He didn't take me seriously...until I called the shelters and asked whether or not I could bring my cat and rabbit with me. Of course the answer was no and I didn't feel right leaving the innocent animals with a clearly unstable and malicious father. I knew I couldn't trust him to take care of them.

Even though Father knew I wasn't going to move out, he realized that he was losing me, at least the obedient side of me, that is. Seeking control, he knew in order to keep me obedient like he wanted, he would have to come up with a plan, as he always did.

Fate worked out in his favor. Later that week while driving to therapy, I looked down for a second, and my car tire hit a pothole. The car was still drivable but needed to go into the shop again. It was getting to the point where the car was at the mechanic's place more than it was at mine.

Realizing this and seizing the opportunity that had so clearly presented itself to him, Father told me, "I've been thinking. Your car repairs will cost over $1,000, which is a lot, especially when you include the money we've already put into it. It really doesn't make sense to keep that car."

Remembering the aforementioned money struggles, I was assuming that Father's words meant that I would soon be without a car.

My freedom was nice while it lasted. I guess there's no more escaping him now. Hello, misery!

Instead, Father continued with, "Now, Mom doesn't think we should just *buy* you a car, but it's not like you can work, so how else would you get one? She thinks it's a bad idea, but I keep trying to convince her."

Remembering his previous comment about how we supposedly didn't have enough money for me to go out to eat with my friend, I found this odd and had come to realize that Father was a chronic liar. However, knowing that I had no escape without a car, and that I couldn't hold down a job while living with Father, I chose not to question him, and simply go along with his little game.

Although I realized that much, I had yet to realize that Father's intention was to further drive a wedge between Mother and I, making him my preferred parent. I had yet to realize it but turning me against Mother would have more than one benefit to him; it would also reestablish my obedience.

Eventually, after much convincing toward Mother, Father drove me to a local car dealership and signed a contract to purchase a brand-new car for me.

Driving around in something new made me feel halfway classy for once. I was used to being broke. Father counted on this, obviously. He made it a point to remind me several times that he had bought me a brand-new car, and that "You owe me big time!"

Father knew his big expenditure and constant reminders would make me feel obligated to keep him around, thus keeping me inside that house despite his abuse. After all, it's not like he had a choice at this point. If he allowed me to move to a shelter, people might think less of him He had led them all to believe that I was autistic. What kind of father would allow his autistic daughter to move to a homeless shelter?

I may as well accept his charity since he's right, I can't work. And who would even want to be with someone who can't work? Plus, it's not like I can do anything right anyway. What's the point in even trying?

My church group announced that we were all invited to go to the concert of a Christian band that was coming to town. I never listened to that kind of music, but decided I wanted to go anyway, for the social aspect.

We all met at the church, then rode together on the church bus to the event. I enjoyed the concert and took lots of pictures, feeling normal for just a few hours. On the way home, they were doing road work on the exit that led to my house, so I had to bypass that exit and take the next one.

Unfortunately, because of construction traffic, there was congestion. I was at a standstill, exhausted, impatient, and more than ready to go home to bed. Out of nowhere, there was a very loud noise and an obvious impact as something hard inside my seat was jabbed into my lumbar area. I was disoriented and unsure of what had happened, but eventually looked up to see that a vehicle had collided with my car.

In the midst of all this, a passerby had stopped to the left of me and rolled down his window, so I rolled mine down.

He asked, "Are you alright?"

In a state of shock, I really didn't know, but responded with, "Yeah, I think so." I paused, then added, "Thanks for stopping." I honestly was surprised that anyone cared to stop at all. Then I asked, in desperate need of companionship during that moment, "Please don't leave." I didn't want to be alone in that moment and really didn't want to have to call Father. I knew he was going to be pissed and I really didn't want to put up with him.

"I won't," the stranger kindly responded to my request.

I looked down quickly in search of my phone, but discovered that it had been thrown from the impact. I reached for the charging cord, which I then used to reel my phone up to me. Thankfully it was still connected. I dialed 911, then peered up in the direction of the kind stranger to see that he had driven off, thus further spurring my abandonment issues. Damn dude, you couldn't stick around for five minutes??

When the police arrived, the man who had been driving the truck that had slammed into me ran back to his car. I told the officer my story, then called Father. I was obviously still shaken up. I had awakened him out of a deep slumber, yet it didn't take him long to arrive at the scene since I was so close to home.

Upon arrival, the officer and Father both disbelieved my story that the man had been driving the truck, not his wife, as the couple were claiming. Even worse, when I mentioned to the policeman that I had PTSD (a diagnosis I had been given due to living with Father), he stared blankly at me as if to assume I was not a credible witness.

Stupid cop! PTSD makes it so I am a better witness than most, dumb ass! Your job is to protect and serve, not scare people into feeling like police officers won't help them or disbelieve when they need it most! I know I'll never call law enforcement again. I can't trust anyone who is so quick to judge. And I can't trust any agency that would hire such an arrogant person.

When Father saw the people who had driven the truck into my vehicle, he grew angry and quickly started walking towards them, malice showing on his face.

"Dad!" I yelled. While I was so proud to have a Father who wouldn't let anyone give me hell (I secretly wanted to punch these people myself), I was simultaneously embarrassed at having a father who was stupid enough to be doing this in front of a policeman, of all people.

The policeman told Father to stop, putting his hand up as if directing traffic. Driven by rage, Father persisted until the officer offered a second warning, this time, his other hand about to unholster his gun. Father paused, noticing this, and then chose not to proceed.

My car was in the shop for two weeks. The other people's insurance company paid for the repairs and were very apologetic about the inconvenience it had caused, even admitting that the man's wife wasn't even on the policy, so they thought that he had actually been the one driving.

"See!" I told Father. "I told you!" Finally, someone to tell him I wasn't crazy.

I wish that stupid cop could hear them say that!

I ended up realizing a few days later that there was a problem. I was in pain. Thankfully the insurance company also agreed to pay for massage therapy for my back. I wouldn't have to hear from Father how much money I was costing him for that too. I started getting massages on a regular basis and even signed up for the year-long package, knowing that it didn't matter that I was broke since the insurance company would have to pay for it.

The insurance company sent us a letter offering a settlement, which I told Father I would not sign. They were only offering $1,600 for my pain and suffering. Father began pressuring me to sign the paper, saying that if I didn't sign the settlement, I wouldn't get anything, which I knew was untrue. He usually left me alone, but, seeing dollar signs, he continually entered my room twice a day for the next two weeks, each time pressuring me to sign the settlement. I continued to refuse, but each visit he paid me had more insults and curses.

Eventually, after two weeks of this harassment, I couldn't take it any more. Tired of hearing him say, "God damn it, Eliza! Just sign the fucking thing!", and afraid of what he might do to me if I kept refusing, I agreed to sign it.

I said, "But only if you pay for my massages afterward, since there is still a problem."

"Fine," he said annoyedly.

Later on, my back was still hurting, and I was diagnosed with early onset arthritis due to the car accident. The doctor recommended massage therapy to help with pain and maintaining mobility.

I suspected that Father would complain about the money he would have to spend since the money from the settlement had run out, but took solace in the fact that he couldn't do anything about it since I had signed a legal agreement for services with the massage parlor.

A few days later, Father came to me and told me that I wouldn't be going to massage therapy anymore because we couldn't afford it.

"I can't not go," I responded. "For one, you promised to pay for the sessions since you forced me to sign a settlement I didn't want to sign. Plus, we're locked into the agreement with the massage parlor."

"Not anymore," Father responded coyly.

"What are you talking about?" I questioned. "Why would they be willing to break a legally binding document?"

"I talked to the manager and told her that your therapist threatened you to get you to sign up for an entire year. She told me that the therapist had been fired, and then apologized profusely and canceled the contract."

Appalled at Father's devious actions, I impulsively shouted, "What?!! Why would you do that?" He didn't to care. He didn't answer me.

"You know that's not true!" I continued. "She has a young daughter to support, which she can't do if she's fired! What if word gets around about that rumor and she becomes unhireable?!"

"Tough titties," he responded icily.

I was both stunned and mortified at his complete lack of empathy. *What the fuck! I'm living with a criminal!*

At home, away from Father's earshot, I told Mother what he had done, thinking that this time she would finally realize how bad her husband truly was. Instead of being appalled, as expected, she offered the usual, "He shouldn't have done that."

I reminded her of it again the next night, to which she replied, "I don't remember that."

That's when I realized how wrapped around Father's little finger Mother really, truly was.

Now more than ever, I knew it was time to get out, while I still had a chance.

With his complete lack of empathy, he'll probably kill me if I piss him off. Especially since he's talked about how he thought the neighbor's daughter should be shot.

Feeling obligated to keep Father around meant continuing to stay in that abusive environment, as did being unable to work. Although I had previously thought it impossible for me to have any more problems, remaining in that situation caused yet another issue.

After Father yelled at me one day, Mother entered my room to find me staring blankly. She began talking to me but I couldn't hear a thing. I continued to stare blankly at nothing. After a few minutes, Mother realized that I was unresponsive to words, or even hand motions.

Frantically she started waving her hands in front of my face, and raised her voice, "Eliza! Eliza!"

After several long minutes, my brain suddenly became functional again. I was startled to see Mother in my room.

"Whoa," I gasped, pausing, then saying, "When did you get here?"

This happened twice in one week, which Mother brought up to the therapist, obviously concerned.

"It was almost as if she were comatose!" Mother emphasized, fear in her voice.

My therapist paused before offering an explanation, seemingly aware that Mother might not fully comprehend it.

"That phenomenon is called disassociation," my therapist explained. "It happens when a situation is too much for a person to handle. It's the brain's way of protecting them from their painful reality."

"Okay," Mother said, seemingly waiting for further explanation. She was clearly missing the point.

Realizing this, as was her job, the therapist added, "Eliza can't handle her environment and her brain knows this, so her brain has to create an escape in order for Eliza to be able to cope."

Even after that, Mother continued to make excuses for him and accepted disassociation as a new part of my daily problems. This became a part of my new normal.

Although Mother was oblivious, it was obvious to both my therapist and myself that she had completely missed the point of the therapist's explanation.

Really, Mom?! Both I and my therapist have told you countless times TO YOUR FACE that Father is the problem, that I need to get away from him, that you put him on a pedestal, and now this? I was barely able to function before, and now I have another problem that HE caused, and, yet again, you completely miss the point? You can't put two and two together, even when we spell it out for you!

What did I do to deserve a birth mother that didn't want me, and a second mother who won't help me or defend me? What did I do to deserve her caring more about her husband than about me? I'm supposedly her daughter but she certainly doesn't act like it. I know she settled for me, and really wanted a biological child, but really?!

Finally, after several years, a date had been set for my social security disability hearing. I was so excited. I figured it would be granted since I really needed it, and then I could get away from Father. This had to be a sure thing! Father and Mother had sought out a lawyer. The best part was that they wouldn't have to pay unless we won the case, meaning that our lawyer would have to ensure that we won so she would be paid.

Before the hearing, I had nothing but excitement, anticipating my new-found freedom from the abuse. I hadn't been aware that Father and I shared a joint bank account, which I would discover later.

To ensure that I had proof of severe depression, I had created videos of my breakdowns and anxiety attacks after I had applied for disability years ago.

"I have videos of depression," I told the lawyer proudly, feeling for once like I could halfway take care of myself.

"You don't need to show them any of that," she responded.

Her comment instantly caused me to question her abilities.

Why would anyone give me money based on my claims alone? The judge doesn't know me. Anyone can go in and act like they can't work.

Even with my bad mental state, I knew that courts operate on proof and don't simply take someone at their word unless they can exhibit evidence.

During the hearing, the judge asked questions about how often it affected me, and it was clear that it didn't sit well with him that Father cut me off mid-sentence, as he scolded Father for interrupting me.

Of course, Father offered a fake "Sorry" as a formality.

Against my better judgement, I neglected to show any of the proof. I knew that lawyer would be sorry later when Father yells at her for making us wait even longer for a retrial. When the trial drew to a close, the judge looked at me coldly and said, "You just got it made, don't you?"

I was shocked. *What the fuck?*

"It must be nice sitting around all day watching TV, living off your parents dime," the judge continued bluntly.

Used to Father's theory of being seen and not heard, I was too afraid to speak out. Instead of defending myself, I just sat there and continued to be slighted by a federal court judge.

You arrogant prick! You're sitting there all high and mighty! YOU try this shit. Watch TV shows 'til you're bored out of your fucking skull. Watch your classmates and friends on social media as they all have lives because they're able to work. Watch them all go out with friends, meet someone to love them, travel the world...not struggle to breathe, not hate their life. No wonder you're a judge. That's all you know how to do. Fuck you and the high horse you rode in on! I hope you die in a car crash, a slow, painful death! I wasn't getting that disability after all.

During my nightly fight with Mother, I shouted, yet again, the same memories and flaws about Father that she continually refused to see. And, yet again, she replied, "I don't remember that."

"You never do!" I shouted. "That's the problem! You're part of the problem! Why can't you see that he's a very bad person? I hate him! He's the most repulsive, repugnant person I've ever met!"

"E-li-za!" Mother yelled. "Don't you *ever* say that! You shouldn't feel that way! That is *your* daddy and he does *a lot* for you!"

"What?!" I pleaded, begging her to finally see the light. "What does he do?!"

"He pays your bills..." Mother exclaimed, yet her voice trailed off as she was clearly searching for another bullet point to add to the list.

After pausing to allow her an opportunity to try and offer another positive quality about him, I continued, "What else?"

Again she offered, "He does *a lot* for you!"

"Like what?" I asked again, pointlessly.

"He pays your bills..."

"Other than that!" I continued my voice straining to get louder, although I'm not sure why I even tried.

"He pays your bills..." she sounded like a broken record, as if that was the only thing she had been programmed to say. It wasn't until later that I realized that she really had been programmed. She had been programmed by Father's manipulative tactics to only think and say what he wanted her to. I would come to realize that she had already endured seventeen years of that programming before I even came along, which in hindsight, was the variable that led to my wasted time and efforts.

"Other than paying my bills," I pleaded, desperately searching for the mother I had known her to be as a child, hoping and praying that she was still in there somewhere. "Other than that, what does he do for me?"

"He does a lot for you," was her automatic response. It was then I started realizing just how far gone she had become. *He's been working on her for far too long....*

When I once requested an automated mother, that is not at all what I had in mind. She sounded like a record player, so she should've at least been able to play me some badass music.

After years of Father's abuse, Mother's inability to realize the truth, and Father deliberately turning everyone against me, I had reached my breaking point. I had been trying for so long just to hang on, feeling like a string much better left to fray. I had tried everything I could, but just couldn't bear any more.

Father had made me beyond miserable. I was to the point where I no longer had any quality of life. I had no more will to live.

Mother and Father had both come up to my room. I had called Mother to tell her this, hoping that she would finally take me seriously.

I hoped that this would be the last plea I ever had to make. I prayed that Mother would finally start doing more than just listening and then forgetting everything I ever told her.

When they entered my room, I already had a large knife in my hand. Wanting to be done with the agony that never ceased, I didn't hesitate to place the blade near my throat, knowing that with one slice, it could all be over.

Mother's eyes widened as she watched in horror, instantly grabbing the knife in attempt to save me.

After Mother's constant excuses for him and inability to remember any of the trauma I regularly shared with her, I had come to question whether or not I even mattered to her.

At that moment, with the knife to my jugular, I peered into her eyes, searching for any kind of sign at all that she cared about me, any sign that I actually mattered to her. I recognized in her eyes a deep fear, the fear of losing me.

A feeling of relief washed over me as I saw this in her, feeling a sense of worth for a change, just for a split second.

"Paul!" Mother pleaded to her husband as they both stood in front of me.

Everything was happening so fast. I realized in that millisecond that Mother was not strong enough to prevent the blade from piercing my skin. Then I recognized from her pleading tone of voice that she was having to *ask* Father to stop me from ending my life.

Curious as to how Father really felt about me, I peered into his eyes. I was horrified at the look of obvious disgust that I saw in his eyes as they stared back at me. In that moment, a huge piece of me died inside as my heart seemed to sink deep within my body and just disappear.

As the seconds passed on, Father still hadn't even attempted to stop me. Through Father's eyes, I swear I could hear his thoughts, and to this day, I can still hear those words as clearly as a shard of glass piercing me straight through the heart.

His eyes seemed to say, "Go ahead, do it, you piece of shit. I'm so tired of dealing with you. And I never even wanted you anyway!"

I had known that Father had a slew of issues, and that he was very unempathetic, but this was a new shock to the system. I had always believed that somewhere within his cold heart was a man who, deep down, really did care about me. That day, however, I discovered otherwise. That was the day I came to believe that the man who raised me was completely void of any empathy whatsoever. I believe that he is not capable of feeling anything but hate towards anyone. I believe that everything he does is done for his own personal gain, and that he always has an ulterior motive for any nice or thoughtful action.

That day left me feeling more worthless than ever.

I can't even "human" correctly. No one cares enough to even try to see the truth. I really must be completely worthless. I really CAN'T do anything right. I can't even kill myself correctly.

Swearing off any religion and any more conversations with God, I became an atheist. I embraced my feelings of hatred and decided that isolation was the only safe way to live. I thought about all the family friends, acquaintances, and especially the supposed friends I had met at church. They had all abandoned me. I hated the people I met from church the most. They had refused to practice what they literally were preaching. *Total hypocrites!*

I felt that if I let anyone in ever again, they would fall far short of my expectations and would only hurt me in the long run, just as everyone else already had.

After all this, now I find out there is no God. God would not allow this kind of suffering, and for so long! Only someone who had had an easy life would believe such foolishness. But I've been through hell, so I know the truth. Hell is here on earth with all these worthless horrible human beings that only care about themselves. And since there's no God, suicide definitely isn't a sin...

I envisioned how nice it would be to be free from the immense never-ending pain I constantly felt. *The gift of death is the only way out of the curse of life.*

I drove to a gas station and bought my first pack of cigarettes, wishing to be done with life but terrified to attempt suicide again, believing that I wasn't lucky enough to have my suffering ever end. It was my hope that the cancer sticks would help me be done with life and sooner rather than later. *I'm allergic to smoke and have asthma. Yep, this oughta speed things up.*

I knew of course that Father was Mother's confidant; that there wasn't a single thing she wouldn't share with him. I hated it but the reality of my situation was that Mother could no longer think on her own. She had been taught to run everything by him. I knew I couldn't share anything personal with her unless she were to finally see the light and divorce him.

While that part of the situation was agonizing, there was a time in which I was able to use that to my advantage. Already headed down a very steep and troubled path, (evident by the self-mutilation practice cuts I was making on my skin as well as the cigarettes, both of which I was successfully hiding), I continued to fight with both Mother and Father on a daily basis, sometimes more than once.

Father's constant prying was growing increasingly annoying, especially because I had since learned that it was not supposed to be happening. What I really couldn't tolerate were his constant insults and the threats. He knew he controlled my money and I knew as well as he did how much I hated that about myself.

All I wanted was a sense of peace, but felt that it was unattainable. Tired of being abused and battered, one day I just snapped. Remembering that Father was her confidant, and that instance when I had stood up to him in the car, I debated about adding something new to my nightly argument with Mother about Father's abuse.

Maybe she will put me on a pedestal the way she does with Father and tell him, "She didn't mean it" for a change. Or maybe she will be afraid of me like she often seems to be and report me to the police. Father's not worth jail time. ... Then again, its not like I have anything else going for me. Plus he was afraid of me when I stood up to him in the car, so he might have been afraid and heeded the warning... And I really don't have anything else to lose even if Mother does report me to the police. Jail would be better than here. Shit, ANYTHING would be better than here.

I decided to go ahead with my ploy. "I can't stand him!" I cut Mother off before she could offer her usual rebuttal. "He's a horrible person and I hate him more than anything! He knows what he's doing but he just doesn't care!"

She was clearly about to make the usual excuses for him, but I intentionally cut her off again. "If he doesn't stop being an ass, I'm going to strangle him in his sleep!"

Even though I had already considered murdering Father, (I concluded that it was probably the only way I would ever be free of his abuse unless he was in a horrible accident) I realized that there was no way I could ever go through with it. I knew I could never watch the life drain out of someone's eyes. I hoped that Father seriously questioned whether I would actually do it or not, and later figured that he must have. He spoke to me a lot less after that and started to keep more to himself.

Age 28

Father was complaining about his younger brother, who he rarely got along with. He told me that when he and Mother had gone down to visit Grandma, his brother was being an ass and wouldn't shut up. He said that he and his brother were outside on the porch, away from Mother and Grandma, so, while everyone wasn't watching, he had threatened to punch his brother out. He seemed proud to be telling me this, as if he really thought that that was the right way to behave.

What the hell is wrong with him? This is his idea of bragging? What the hell is wrong with him?

Instantly, I was ashamed of having a father that was so violent, cruel, and arrogant. I was even more ashamed feeling that I had no choice but to put up with him.

Although I was an atheist, I continued to attend my church group because the other members had become my friends. A few of these members knew that I was merely attending for the camaraderie at that point, and I was surprised that they didn't try to push their religion onto me.

It was well known within the group that one of our members had been battling cancer for the past several years and we used to end the group with prayers on her behalf. Over the last several months, she had grown increasingly more frail and had even passed out once during a gathering that I had not been able to attend.

Everyone in the group said they would pray for her healing, to which one of my closest friends within the group stated, "Keep in mind that sometimes when God heals people, he brings them home."

That is a more reasonable statement than most religious people make, which is why I still come here. Most fully believe that God will overcome any obstacle, even when its clearly statistically impossible. Why do religious people always have to naïvely look on the bright side of things?

Three weeks after that, our group was notified that our friend had lost her battle with cancer.

Great! What else could go wrong? Yet again, one of my only friends died, and after I only got to go out with her a few times! This is just further proof that there is no God. What God would allow the death of the few people that actually don't abandon me, and so shortly after I met them?!

Knowing how severe my allergies were, my parents had told me countless times that I was not allowed to have a dog. All I wanted was anyone I could call family. I hadn't referred to my human family as family for several years. I was tired of feeling down constantly and knew that I needed something else to take care of. In my mind, that would be the logical first step to eventually being able to take care of myself.

Deliberately turning off the location on my phone, I drove to the shelter and adopted a dog anyway, realizing that neither parent really knew what was best for me. When I arrived back home, I told them immediately that I had done it anyway and that they would just have to deal with it.

What are they gonna do about it? They know taking her back would push me over the edge and neither one of them will want to deal with me at that point. They wouldn't dare rock the boat!

I loved my new dog and deeply enjoyed caring for her. She provided me a reason for existence like I knew it would. Although I developed a need for an entire box of tissues per day due to my constant hay fever, it was worth it for the love I wasn't otherwise receiving in my own home, as well as the companionship that I so desperately needed.

To this day, I'm still surprised that no one ever equated the need for a companion despite severe allergies with covert abuse behind closed doors.

I had come to know my psychiatrist and therapist quite well. They had become a constant in my life. I had been seeing the psychiatrist for thirteen years, and the therapist for eight. One of my only forms of socialization, I had even come to refer to both of them as friends.

One day, my parents claimed they were unsure of when my next appointment with the psychiatrist was. I found it odd, as Mother was notorious for keeping track of doctors' appointments, but didn't even think to question it. When I called to find out when the appointment was scheduled, the receptionist hesitated, sounding uncomfortable. She then awkwardly informed me that I was no longer a patient of their practice.

Shocked, I hung up angrily, believing this was Father's doing. He had previously said, "They don't seem to be helping you since you're never getting any better." Given his previous heartless tactics, this would be right up his alley to call the practice and cancel services, then convince Mother that it was in my best interest.

This is ridiculous! I barely get any socialization, and he takes this from me?! He knows how depressed I am and knows I need that!

Upon confrontation, however, Mother told me that removing me from their practice was the therapists idea. In disbelief, I proceeded to start yelling. Before I could get many words out, Father interrupted me, saying "We wouldn't do that to you. We know how much you were relying on them."

He must've sensed my skepticism, as he began rifling through the never ending mound of crap on the counter. After a few minutes, he unearthed the envelope he was looking for among one of Mother's many piles of hoarded materials. He handed it to me so I could see for myself.

"What the fuck?!" I exclaimed after reading the letter written on the company's letterhead. The practice claimed that they didn't think they were helping me, and were no longer able to extend their services to me since I had canceled too many appointments.

"But the therapist told me that talking about my trauma too much was hurting me and that I needed a break!" I exclaimed in shock and offense.

"I know," offered Mother sympathetically. "I remember them telling you that." *Yeah, that you remember!*

"How can they do this to me?" I exclaimed. "They said they loved me!" As the years went on, I would go on to notice several so-called "red-flags" about that practice in particular, including the comment listed above.

Instantly, I was filled with rage and hatred. All the previous feelings of abandonment resurfaced. This time, the sting was so much worse. I had known those people so much longer than the friends who had discarded me over the years.

Even worse, the psychiatrist continued to refuse to refill my medication even though I was unable to find a new doctor before the scripts ran out. Luckily, my general practitioner agreed to write me the scripts I needed so that I could continue getting my medications. We later found out that my body had become addicted to those particular medications. If my general practitioner hadn't written my scripts, my body could've gone into shock from withdrawals and I could've been hospitalized or even died.

It took my family two years of attempting to find a new psychiatrist and therapist before we found a place that would actually accept me. Every practice we met with said, "If they can't help you, I don't know what we can do." It got to the point that I didn't want to tell anyone else who I had been seeing because I knew they wouldn't help me.

This is just great, I'm obviously beyond help. Suicide really is the only option I have. No one cares about me anyway. If anyone did, some practice would care enough to accept me.

It was official, I had entered a new level of pathetic. Before, I had been thrown away on a personal level. This time, however, I had been discarded professionally. Maybe I should've worn a name tag that said "Professional Trash Bag."

Sick and tired of abuse but unable to work due to severe anxiety and depression, I began thinking that the only way out was to find a man to support me. With not having a healthy Mother and no one who had stepped up to help me, dependency was the only example set for me. Because of this, it never occurred to me that maybe I could do things if I gave it a try. I used to believe that but both Mother and Father had done a bang up job proving to me that that wasn't true. They had instilled in me that I wasn't capable of much. Even when I had done my best, it wasn't good enough. My parents, as well as employers, frequently told me to "try harder." I hated that. Try harder. I'm trying way harder than anyone else around me!

I'm doing the best I can. It's all I can do just to function each day. It takes so much energy just to get up off the couch. I hated how everyone mistook my severe depression for laziness. *Does anyone know me at all?*

When one has no job and barely leaves the house, it becomes impossible to find a mate. Although I didn't really like the idea, I knew that the only option available to me under such circumstances was to try dating apps. Making it even harder was the fact that the quality apps were all paid, so those obviously weren't an option for someone like me who was flat broke.

But I was desperate to escape the abuse, so I tried the free apps anyway. Most chats came and went or I found that I really didn't have much in common with the person on the other end. Eventually, I started a conversation with a guy and we hit it off. We chatted for hours each day, lasting a duration of nine months, after which time we decided to meet.

My house was my safe haven and I had a fear of leaving it. Obviously not wanting to admit this, I told the guy, "I'm not comfortable leaving right now."

He then asked if he could come to me. The babe in the woods that I was (much like Mother) it didn't even occur to me how that could've been perceived.

Besides, I am obese. Who would be interested in me? Even my own father calls me a fat slob.

Like an idiot, I told him he could come over and then we exchanged information. He said he was on his way over and would be there within the hour.

I went downstairs to inform Father about the impending company. Before I could get it out, he told me he was headed out the door on his way to get some coffee, as he often did. Then I went to inform Mother, who announced that she had plans with her friend, who was on her way to pick her up. I opted not to tell them after all.

I was uneasy about being home alone with this guy I hadn't met in person. Desperate to get out of the abusive environment, I chose to believe that enough bad things had already happened to me for five lifetimes, therefore it was statistically highly improbable that anything else bad would happen. *As much as I've been through, it's way past time for things to start going right in my life.*

Shortly after the man I had met on the dating app arrived, he approached me closely and I was instantly uncomfortable. Before I knew it, he had me against a wall and had swiftly managed to place his hands down my underpants.

"No!" I shouted, realizing I was being completely violated, for the third time! "Stop!" I screamed.

My heart raced as I attempted to push the asshole away, yet despite my obesity, my female body still wasn't strong enough to overpower him. That was when I realized that, since I wasn't strong enough, I was going to be raped this time, not just molested like before.

Luckily, in that moment, it never occurred to me that if he did penetrate me, I could become pregnant with his abomination. The only thing happening in my mind was the acknowledgment of the fear and defeat that I was feeling. I felt weak, insecure, unimportant, powerless, worthless, and extremely guilty.

Suddenly, miraculously, the guy froze. Unsure of what was happening, all I noticed was that he had suddenly stopped. Then I heard the sound of something rumbling. After several long seconds that seemed like minutes, it occurred to me that it was the sound of my wonderful dog, faithfully coming to my rescue. Honestly, I was completely taken aback that she defended me. Ashamedly, I had forgotten that she had even been there.

"What is she doing?" the guy asked, idiotically. "She knows what you're trying to do," I snapped, "and she won't let you." He began backing away from me slowly.

All at once, the culmination of everything I had endured throughout many long years surfaced emotionally. Although many of the memories were still repressed, I felt something inside the back of my mind, on a subconscious level. That event was the final straw that forever changed me. I was beyond done with any and all mistreatments, not just Father's.

Always shy, quiet, and afraid to speak out, I said to the guy forcefully and with a newfound attitude and confidence, "She'll rip your balls off!"

My scare tactic worked. He instantly placed his hands in front of his crotch to guard his precious family jewels. I watched in amazement, honor, and humor as my wonderful little wonder dog kept her guard up, escorting him as he walked backwards slowly and then ran out the door.

As if I needed any more proof that I had made the right decision by adopting her, I now had even more confirmation. I was honored to be that sweet doggy's mother and felt quite lucky that someone cared about me enough to be my family, finally, after all these years of feeling completely alone. I bet not many people can say this: on the bright side, I only got molested... again.

And just like that, everything changed. I had previously viewed my literal walls as my safe space, and felt like nothing bad would happen within that space, even with all the abuse happening. This, however, shattered my entire reality. My safe space was no longer safe; it was heavily contaminated. The space that my mind had once seen when looking around my house was gone now. Within my mind, my walls were torn down. It was almost as if I could see a vast empty space where the walls had been, leaving me feeling vulnerable and exposed...in every sense of the word. My safe space no longer existed and I had no idea how to deal with that.

All I wanted at that given moment was to go to Mother. I knew that she would understand and share my upset and fear, but I also knew that she would then go tell Father, who would no doubt blame me for what happened and then later use the story of that event to discredit me and gain more attention for himself.

Instead, I kept that terrifying night to myself and thanked my wonderful dog. I spent the night imagining how Mother used to be when I had been little and wishing for that version of her now. I imagined how great her embrace would've felt as she held me in her arms while I sobbed in her lap, overcome with grief and fear. But I was finally starting to realize that Mother was different now and that a return to her previous state was unlikely.

Instead, I kept all of those feelings bottled inside. I was afraid to tell anyone because I thought it was all my fault. I would later learn that this is a common reaction.

I should've known better. I echoed Father's words, but in this instance, I truly believed them. *I never should've met with someone I didn't know and definitely not at my house. Maybe I didn't say no loud enough or in the right way. I'm so pathetic only bad guys are interested in me and only just to use me. I'm so fat and ugly that the only way anyone could ever be interested in me is as a toy. I'm ugly and worthless and pathetic and gross. I'm nothing. I'm not strong enough.*

Those last four words kept ringing through my mind. No matter how hard I tried, I couldn't forget those four words. That was all I could hear. Over and over, I heard it.

I'm not strong enough.

It was something I had believed for years, something that had made me feel inferior. It was part of what kept me afraid to venture out of the house, and afraid to socialize. This time, though, those words had started to haunt me. *I'm not strong enough.*

That was when I recovered my first repressed memory. I had been all of five years old when I had prayed to God that He would make me psychic, so I will know when to run and hide when Father was about to get mad. At that young age, it never occurred to me that I didn't deserve it or that I should try to fight back, or that I even could.

Clearly, I was done being nice, done with my childlike innocence, done with anyone or anything that wasn't right. I realized that day what I had been suspecting for a while, that it was up to me to take care of myself because no one else would. And, for the first time ever, I began to realize that I actually did possess value.

During the days that followed, I began leaving my house regularly for the first time in years...to work out at the gym I had just joined. That was the beginning of the end of my abuse. The light at the end of the tunnel. My turning point. The beginning of a new dawn. It was the end of "nothing" and the beginning of everything.

Suicidal ideation was something that had come to afflict me on a daily basis, a problem that most people avoided me for. I felt lucky to have Mother. She would always come sit with me during those painful moments. Anytime I would tell her I wasn't safe, that was the indicator that I was at the end of my rope and couldn't take it anymore. That phrase indicated that I needed immediate intervention in order not to go through with ending my life.

Living with those two people came to be like my battle between the light and darkness, between good and evil. Mother, always the peacemaker and the person who put others first, obviously resembled the light, the good. Father, completely narcissistic and self-centered, was the darkness, the evil. Whereas Mother would always come to my aid during suicidal times, Father had come to completely ignore me, *especially* during the suicidal times. He had all but washed his hands of me and I knew that he despised everything about me.

It was nothing out of the ordinary when I called Mother for the millionth time, saying, "I'm not safe."

Tired of it all, it was obvious that she had had enough. She replied, "I can't sit with you right now. I already sat with you once today."

Pausing in shock, I eventually asked, "Did you not hear what I just said? I'm not safe!"

"Eliza, we are tired of this," she answered coldly.

Appalled, I proceeded, "Do you not even care if I die?"

"I can't keep being at your constant beck and call!" she responded.

"You always say you need me," I replied. "Now I realize that it isn't true. Now I know you were just saying that."

Mother didn't seem to hear any of what I had said.

"Your dad and I have things we want to do too," she continued. "We had plans to travel around the world, but we can't even enjoy ourselves because we're always taking care of you!"

That was the first of many instances of her sounding like Father.

"What the hell, Mom!" I yelled. "I told you that the only reason I am even still here is because you say you need me and want me here. I've been nothing but miserable for years and only kept on existing for you! If I had known that you felt this way, I would've killed myself years ago!"

I paused, desperately hoping that she would see the error in her ways, but she said nothing.

In complete disbelief at the only family member I had turning on me, I said, "Fine, if this is how you feel, go ahead and live it up. Go on your vacations and live a life I can never have. You'll have plenty of time soon, 'cause I'll be dead. You won't have to deal with the burden of me anymore. You guys can finally enjoy life once I'm gone." Then I hung up on her.

She had broken my heart several times before, but this was worse. Now, my entire world is shattered.

Afraid to even admit this to myself, I was hoping that Mother would realize that I was serious and call me back and try to stop me. Extreme disappointment set in after a few minutes when she never did.

How could she not realize that she's already broken my heart numerous times before? How does she not realize that she was my entire world? Now that I know she feels this way, I'm left with nothing. The only reason I hadn't committed suicide yet had just given me the go ahead to finally do so.

This was a new pain that I had never felt before and it hurt worse than anything else I had ever experienced. It had been bad enough that Mother refused to see the truth about Father, but now even she didn't care about me. I just needed to matter to anyone at all. This was the first time I ever felt completely worthless to every single person on the planet. In that moment, I fully believed that there wasn't a single person who would even care if I died.

Even Rose is just being nice to me to be polite. I bet she doesn't even care.

I needed a reason not to end my miserable life. I was terrified to attempt suicide again but felt that it was my only option. I needed a reason not to...any reason at all...but I couldn't find a single one.

I'm such a burden. Everyone told me that they need and want me here, but if that was true, they would all be here with me now, telling me that again instead of leaving me alone when they know I'm about to kill myself.

It didn't occur to me until later that Father had probably convinced people that I was exaggerating, so they probably believed that I was not serious, even though I was more serious than ever before.

Over the years I realize that Father had probably convinced Mother to respond in that manner. It hadn't occurred to me, and definitely hadn't occurred to her either, that with her being the only one trying to do anything to help me, and Father's complete unwillingness to help, every single aspect of my care fell onto her alone. No wonder she was so tired.

I'm done with both of them. No one cares about me at all, so what's the point in continuing on? After all they've put me through it would serve them both right to find my dead body. All she cares about is her perfect husband who can do no wrong. I don't matter at all.

I considered taking a bunch of pills to accomplish the deed, enjoying the idea of being free of agony, finally, after all those years. Just as pleasing was the thought of how great it would be for everyone who knew us to find out that Father really was abusive, which I would make sure to include details about in the note I would leave.

Then it occurred to me that Mother would be the one to find me, and she would show Father my body and the note, and that he would no doubt hide it, like it never happened, to preserve his fake image. Then I grew sick to my stomach as the realization hit me that he would use my death to gain attention and pity from everyone. He would surely make it known that I had killed myself and blame it on my supposed mental illness and autism. He was tired of dealing with me anyway and my death would make him happy. I decided that I would not allow him to use me for his personal gain. Suddenly, I had a great idea: I decided I would do everything within my power to attempt to reacquire a quality of life, just to spite him. I would find a way to move out, no matter what it took, and prove that I didn't need him.

Even still, every day was an uphill battle, and as a result of that painful turn of events, I came extremely close to a second suicide attempt shortly after. I had made yet another raw and honest video for my mental health awareness channel, this time discussing the bottle of pills in my hand that I had almost used for another suicide attempt, yet decided not to, out of fear.

One of the members from my church group had seen this video and took it upon herself to reach out to my parents to try to get me some help. This was one of many individuals who would contact my caregivers, not realizing that they weren't actually caring for me and were instead the very issue causing my problems.

And each time, my parents would thank the individual for reaching out, explain that they had been trying to help me for years, and ask the individual to keep them posted about any updates they knew about me.

Eventually, I began shutting down and distancing everyone because I knew that no one would believe me. I knew that I couldn't trust anyone because they would report back to my parents. Instead of gaining the socialization I needed, that act had caused me to isolate even further.

How am I supposed to ever begin to be okay when everyone is reporting everything I do back to my abusers? Why is everyone so stupid not to realize that there is more than one side to every story? Why can't anyone see that they're making me sick?! No matter what I say, no one will believe me. All I need is one person to allow me the chance to prove myself to them, to prove that I'm not ill or autistic. Why won't anyone pull their head out of their ass long enough to give that to me?

Maybe Father is right. Maybe I really can't do the things I think I might be able to do. I mean, it's not like I haven't tried countless times before. And even when I try my hardest, everyone says I need to "try harder." Obviously, I really can't do anything right. Besides, it's not like I will ever be able to escape this prison of a house. Even if I tried to move out, Father still would never leave me alone. Maybe it is pointless to even try.

At the request of our neighbor Mrs. Robbins, I had begun caring for their aging parents a year or so prior. The father had since passed on, so now I cared solely for the mother, who I had become great friends with. Before I left one day, Mrs. Robbins and I had been chatting, and somehow the subject of my parents arose. Although I had tried to tell countless others the truth many times before, I thought I would try once more.

Being my other family, I spent a lot of time here growing up, so maybe she will realize I'm not the type to make things up...

Yeah, right! I'm not that lucky. At this point I'm so used to disappointment that I've come to expect it. What's one more person who doesn't believe me?

Expecting disbelief as usual, I said casually, "Behind closed doors, things are going on that shouldn't be."

I've said it countless times before with others, so why would this be any different?

"What's going on?" questioned Mrs. Robbins.

I paused, taken aback at the unexpected response.

She's just humoring me to make me feel better. She has to be...right?

"Father insults me and Mother goes along with it," I responded, again expecting some form of rebuttal in disbelief.

"They shouldn't be doing that," she responded, empathetically.

I couldn't believe it, and literally didn't know what to say or even think. So I simply said thank you, grabbed the tool she agreed to lend me, and went home.

Once safely behind the closed door of my room, I sobbed, overcome with emotion. I still couldn't believe that anyone had listened to me, and even better, she had actually believed me! The tears of joy continued to stream down my red, puffy face for the next several minutes. I couldn't believe that after so many years, someone had finally believed *me!*

For the first time in several long years, my feelings had been validated. It was as if the shroud of darkness that had so heavily surrounded my entire life had been lifted, just slightly.

Things were still far from great, but this was a start. The encounter had given me the courage to move forward with my plan to find a way to move out.

Reborn Anew

A^{ge 29}   With my new found confidence, I knew what I had to do. It was no longer just a pipe dream. I needed to distance myself from my living environment to allow myself to heal enough to be able to hold down a job. I had made up my mind. Even though it wasn't ideal, I knew that the only opportunity I had to escape was to move to a homeless shelter.

One day, I packed a light bag and said my goodbyes to my dog, who I vowed to come back to once I found work. I absolutely hated to leave her but was relieved at last to know that she would not be in any danger. Father had grown attached and spoiled her rotten.

My dog had recently passed her test as a service dog so that I could bring her everywhere with me to help with my dissociative PTSD episodes and anxiety attacks. Father grew concerned when he saw that I was leaving with a bag without my faithful companion. I didn't think I'd ever see him concerned for me so I wasn't sure where this was coming from.

"Where are you going?" he questioned. "I'm moving out," I responded confidently for the first time in my entire life. "Where are you going to go?" he asked cockily, clearly believing that he still had the upper hand. "To a homeless shelter," I responded, finally realizing that I actually *was* worth something. "Anywhere is better than here." He didn't argue. He didn't try to stop me.

The address was already entered into my GPS as I walked out the door, tears streaming down my cheeks as I left my faithful companion, but happy for a new beginning. Even though I knew it would be filthy and not at all glorious, I knew it would be better than my current living arrangement. I was proud to move into a filthy environment. I knew that I would be taking my dignity back by doing so.

About half way there my phone rang, the screen indicating that it was Father on the other end of the line. I waited a minute before answering. I assumed that he had called to offer another one of his fake apologies in an attempt to smooth things over and get me to come back.

There is nothing he can say that could make me reconsider.

"Hello?" I answered.

"Hey," he said coolly, attempting to sound unworried. "Mom and I got to talking, and we crunched the numbers and figured out that we could spend about $800 a month to get you your own apartment."

There's nothing he can say to make me reconsider...except that. I was in shock. I knew that he was trying to manipulate me, but I didn't care. *No homeless shelter? My very own place? Hell yeah!*

Only this time, things were going to be done on my terms. Once I had had enough time away from him, I would be able to work, and then I could completely sever ties.

Within a few months, a place had opened up for me and I moved in. It was in a low rent apartment complex, of course, but I didn't care that it wasn't the greatest area. The apartment was mine...all mine. The best part was the fact that someone else, my abusers nonetheless (*even better*), were paying for it. It was as if they were starting to pay for all the wrongs they put me through.

My apartment. What a lovely sound! Freedom!!

It was the only place where I could not be insulted or berated, but also so much more. It was my first real taste of independence. Although they were paying for it, I finally lived by myself, safe from his abuse, safe to express myself, to have my own thoughts, to have my own feelings, and to finally express either one of them freely. Freely without judgement, without being told what to do, without being told what to think or that I was incorrect for thinking or feeling the way I did.

The elation didn't last long, however. Father would randomly show up unannounced and use his key to let himself in. I hadn't wanted him to have a key but knew I couldn't say no. After all, he was paying for it so I was obligated. He made sure to often remind me of that fact.

He showed up at least once a day, watching TV and playing games on his phone. It was like he just wanted to harass me while simultaneously escaping Mother. *This is supposed to be mine!*

I came to regret choosing the apartment over the homeless shelter. I would barricade myself in my bathroom, just so I didn't have to be exposed to the toxicity of Father's judgmental, derogatory comments. This is what I was trying to escape! Then I would call Mother telling her that I was uncomfortable and that he needed to leave. After much prodding, she would call him and ask him to come home.

During one of those visits, I had the gumption to call my friend from my church group who had taken me under her wing and pointed out that my living situation wasn't normal.

I told her that Father was there again and that I was uncomfortable. She knew the truth and that I was in denial.

She asked again the same thing she had asked before, "Has he ever been physical with you?"

Overcome with fear and grief, I finally responded honestly, "Yes." As I cried, she and I both knew that I had finally been honest with myself. Suddenly, I heard Father at the door. My heart began racing even faster.

Shit! He's been listening! Now I'm really gonna get it!

I didn't know what to do but I refused to hang up the phone. I just wished that someone other than myself or Mother would finally hear him.

Then he said, "What are you doing in there?"

"I'll be out in a minute," I said, relieved that he had apparently not been listening at the door and seemed unaware of my phone conversation.

"Hurry up, I have to take a shit," he raised his voice angrily.

Knowing that my eyes were red from crying, I didn't want to leave the bathroom knowing that he would realize what I had been doing. He kept persisting, and eventually I exited the bathroom, my heart pounding as I still kept my friend on the other end of the line, making sure to keep the phone screen down so Father hopefully wouldn't notice.

"It's about time," he grumbled.

When he saw the redness on my face, he added, "God damn it, Eliza! Again with that anxiety shit? Why can't you just learn to deal with things? It's not rocket science."

He closed the door angrily, turned on the fan, then I went into my bedroom and closed the door behind me. Placing the phone to my ear, I asked, "Are you still there?"

"Yes," responded my amazing friend.

Knowing that someone cared enough to remain on the line with me during that panic made her voice sound like the most soothing sound I had ever heard.

"Are you okay?" she questioned.

"Yeah," I responded. "Thanks to you."

After several weeks, I implored Mother to have a talk with Father about not coming over unannounced, something that he had promised he would never do. I made it clear to her that I didn't want him coming over at all. Eventually, after several more weeks, it miraculously sunk into her brain and she was somehow able to convince him to stop visiting me.

For Christmas, I told my parents that I was not going over there for the holiday. Their house was very musty and caused my breathing problems. I finally felt confident enough to put my foot down about that. However, I didn't want to spend Christmas alone so I invited them over to my apartment instead.

I guess being abused for one day would be better than spending my favorite holiday alone.

Father usually didn't like being anywhere other than his house, so they only stayed for about a half hour, leaving me alone and suicidal afterward. I told Mother that I would be suicidal if they left, but yet again, it didn't seem to matter to her.

"Daddy doesn't like being away from home," she said.

"And I don't like being alone and suicidal!" I retorted.

"You're welcome to come over to our house," she responded.

"I told you," I responded, "I can't breathe from the mold in that house."

The comment seemed to go over her head, and they left, ignoring my deteriorating emotional state.

Attempting another plea for help, I took to Facebook, posting, "Here I am, all alone on Christmas because no one cares."

One of their friends responded to my post saying that I should go home for Christmas because "that's what most people do."

Not caring what anyone thought or who found out the truth, I responded publicly, "I can't go home. I'm allergic to their house."

Their friend responded, "You're not allergic to that house. Just go home and be with your family."

I wasn't at all surprised at their friend's reaction. She was another one of their people who never seemed to understand that there is always more than one side to every story.

Instead of going home, I drove to their next door neighbors' house to be with my elderly friend who I had cared for and spent the rest of Christmas with her.

Later, I found out that Father had used his manipulation tactics again. One of his friends texted me saying, "I'm glad you decided to go home for Christmas." *Puke*. Actually I wasn't even there and never saw my so-called parents. Of course Father would tell people that. It would look bad if he told them the truth that I was never there. I knew any response would be futile, so I ignored the text completely.

At least I have my elderly friend to be with on the holidays from now on.

Months later, however, that friend succumbed to old age and passed away.

Great! Another friend is gone. Guess I'll spend the holidays alone from now on.

Ironically the opportunity did actually arise to marry a man to live off of, just as I had told Mother I would do just to get away from them. He was an older man who lived in my apartment complex. While I hated our nearly twenty year age difference, I was miserable and knew that more than anything, I needed to have a way to sever ties with Father and Mother. He had expressed interest in me and had even offered to take care of me. I seriously considered marrying the man. I knew I was only considering it because I wanted to get away from Father and Mother and that I was using the man, but I didn't care. I considered the idea for several weeks.

Getting married would be easy but I assume that getting unmarried would be really difficult. He might make it hard to get away if I decide I want a divorce later, especially since I would only marry him for the money. What if he was secretly abusive too? What if he treated me like meat? He would obviously be expecting sex from me and I really don't want to do that, especially not with someone I barely know. But even if he made me unhappy, it couldn't be any worse than dealing with Father. Maybe I would get lucky and he would become uninterested in me but I could still reap the benefits financially. I really don't want to be tied down, but it's not like I would be able to find anyone else. Who would want to be with someone who can't even hold down a job?

These thoughts kept running through my brain for several more weeks, but in the end, I opted against marrying the man. I refused to settle for something less than my ideal.

A few weeks later, a member of my church group had invited me over to her house where I had the opportunity to meet one of her other friends, who was also her colleague.

While there, I discussed how life had grown increasingly harder. I was struggling to remember to buy food from the store, forgetting certain self-care activities, and had acquired depth perception issues. I told them that the psychiatrist I was now seeing was actually honest with me, unlike my previous one, who had hidden from me the fact that I had become addicted to most of the medications. This new psychiatrist was on board with helping me to wean off of my medications, which had caused these new challenges.

"Apparently," I told my friend and her coworker, "The potential side effect of 'altered brain chemistry' means brain damage!"

What a nice way to find out that antidepressant and anti-anxiety medications really aren't good for the body!

My friend and her coworker, who were both social workers, were concerned that I was having so much trouble.

"If you're not remembering groceries and struggling with self-care, why do you live alone?" she asked.

"Because my parents are abusive, they don't care about my mental or physical health," I responded, "and I just can't live with them ever again."

"If you are having that much trouble with daily activities," my friend's coworker chimed in, "you should be in assisted living."

In denial, I responded with, "I don't want to live that way. I want to be independent."

Before I ended the visit, they gave me contact numbers of places I could potentially stay that would provide me with the help I needed. Originally having been extremely excited about visiting my friend, I left her house feeling more depressed and hopeless than ever before.

Determined not to live that way and appalled at what the medication had done to me, I decided I would do whatever it took to get sober off of every single prescription and that I would figure out a way to maintain my independence. I swore off any and all unnatural substances, vowing never to take any man-made chemical containing pharmaceuticals ever again.

Besides, telling Mother about any of this information means she will tell Father, who will no doubt blab to everyone what happened and that I need their constant care now. I won't give him the opportunity to use what he indirectly caused to HIS advantage. I'm done letting him exploit me!

This was yet another critical moment that I knew I would have to keep to myself. I spent months away from my parents, enjoying peace for the first time in years. However, living in an empty apartment with no other people was quite hard for me. Needing a break from that and missing Mother, I decided to go visit her and Father one day.

Shortly after I arrived, it was obvious that Mother was angry. She barely spoke to me, which was very unlike her.

"Is everything okay?" I asked.

"No," Mother didn't hesitate to snap at me. "Everything is not okay." Tears began welling up in her eyes.

"What's the problem," I asked, concerned.

Instantly overcome with rage, I was assuming that the problem was that Father had undoubtedly laid a hand on her.

This is it! She's about to break down over something HE did!

Unfortunately, I was met with disappointment yet again.

"Once you moved out, you stopped communicating!" she raised her voice, offended. "We haven't *seen* you, we haven't *heard from* you."

I realized nothing had changed. Mother was still just as sick as she had been before.

"Yeah," I responded, dumbfounded. "I told you that would happen before I left. That I would take any and every opportunity to leave and never look back. Not with him around."

"We're your parents!" she yelled. "*And* we're paying for *your* living expenses!"

"I never asked you to," I responded. "Besides, my church group has noticed how much better I've been now that Father is not around. They agree with the therapist that I need to stay away to preserve my health."

"They said to stay away from *him*," she said, "but what did *I* do?"

Seriously?!! I've only told you five million times!!

"I've only told you five million times!" I said aloud this time. "You allow it!"

"What kind of a church would tell you to turn your back on *your* family?!" she asked.

"People who make someone miserable to the point of being suicidal aren't family," I countered.

"Family are the parents that care for you, love you, and are always there for you," she stated.

"Exactly," I replied. "Neither of you fill that bill. You used to but haven't filled that void for me for years now."

"I am *your Mother*!" she began screaming, "You mean the world to me and I will always take care of you!"

"Then act like it," I replied coldly, realizing that she was pretty far gone at that point.

The look on her face resembled that of a wounded wolf cub, but I didn't care. The amount of pain she had already caused me over many long years far outweighed any pain she felt from my blunt comment.

I walked away from her in disappointment at her sickness and in disgust of Father's obvious brainwashing.

Despite my parents' pleas not to travel to see my grandmother in Florida all alone, I went anyway, with my faithful dog by my side. I really didn't like the idea of traveling alone but had no one to go with other than my parents, who I was avoiding like the plague. Living with Father was bad, but road trips were worse. Road trips meant constant exposure to that toxicity with no barrier, and for hours on end that seemed like months. I felt that any road trip with Father would result in my suicide or his murder. Someone would certainly die on that trip. I wouldn't be able to take that much of him.

And his dumb ass definitely isn't worth jail time!

I texted my friend Deborah, excited about my trip. She had been the one to travel down there with me over a year ago. She was unable to join me this time because she had been experiencing a slew of health issues.

I decided to venture out on my own. It took two days to get there, but the long drive was well worth the escape I got from my boring and pathetic unemployed life. Deborah texted me a few mornings later asking about the trip.

I told her that I was enjoying my vacation and that my dog and I were currently on the island that Deborah and I had ventured to before. She told me she was glad I was enjoying myself, and that the doctors had determined the cause of her latest sickness. She said she was in the car with her dad, who was taking her to the hospital to have the operation needed to remedy the problem.

Having been born with a chronic health condition, Deborah was well accustomed to surgeries and was excited to finally have the problem figured out. She told me that she would text me when she was out of surgery and that she couldn't wait to be her old self again.

I went about the rest of my day, then came home and had a nice dinner with Grandma. I figured that Deborah must be busy texting all of her other friends and must have meant to text me, but forgot. I sent her a message, asking if she was doing okay. After another hour, I messaged her mother since I had her number from when we had been here before.

After my long day, I was exhausted and went to sleep around ten but awoke after one o clock. I looked at my phone, just to see what time it was, and there was a message from her mother on the screen. I wasn't going to read it, but my speed reading brain as well as morbid curiosity, couldn't help but see what it said.

"Hi Eliza, Thanks for reaching out. I want to let you know that Deborah unexpectedly passed away around 8:00 tonight. Her body just couldn't take it anymore. Thanks for your friendship. You were a great friend to her."

I guess it really was a morbid curiosity!

Instantly, the tears welled up in my eyes, and I knew sleep was no longer an option for the night and probably not for the following nights either. It took several hours to sob, allowing all of my grief to surface as I held tightly my beloved dog for the rest of the night.

This is just great. Yet another friend I barely had any time to get to know is dead and gone. I will miss her so much! Why do all my friends die? Please don't let Rose go too!

There was yet another subconscious reason I was afraid to get too close to Rose.

If I get close to her, knowing my luck, she will die, like the rest of my friends! Ugh, this is not what I need right now. Not in the middle of trying to get, and stay, sober. How will I sleep without my anxiety pills after this? How will I not need them just to get through each night?

I was awake for the rest of the night and following day... and most of the following night as well. Determined more than ever not to need the crutch of medication and to overcome the addictions, I decided that not relapsing would be a great way to honor my dear friend, especially since I knew that she wouldn't want her passing to be the reason for my sobriety to fail.

A day after her passing, with little to no sleep, and a plethora of sugary caffeinated soft drinks, (something else I would later remove from my lifestyle) I began the long drive back home, across five state lines.

When I arrived home two days later, even after staying a night in an unfamiliar place, I had, proudly, continued my sobriety journey without taking any of the pills I had brought with me just in case.

Still battling constant loneliness, I turned again to dating apps. I had been chatting with a few men, but one in particular showed an interest in meeting up. He asked what I was doing that day and I informed him I didn't have much going on and that I had just planned to take my dog to the dog park.

He asked if he could meet me there, and I agreed, excited that someone cared enough to join me in my menial day without disrupting it. I was also relieved he didn't try to invite himself to my apartment. I won't ever do that again. A few hours later, we met at the park and hit it off. He chatted with other dog owners that I had gotten to know and paid special attention to my beloved dog. We exchanged numbers and later via text, agreed to meet again.

At our next agreed upon meeting, he was nearly half an hour late and still hadn't arrived. I texted him multiple times with no response. After several more minutes, I assumed I had been stood up, although I found it odd considering he had given me his phone number. He had been texting me so I knew the number was legitimate and he agreed to meet me.

Hours later, I received a response from his phone number. It was a friend of his messaging me. He informed me that the man I had been talking with had passed away. *Are you serious?* Completely taken aback, I asked what happened. The responder claimed that there had been an accident on a pond where they were staying in Illinois.

I didn't respond. I could tell that something wasn't right. For one thing, my date had told me that he would be meeting me after work, which obviously wasn't in a different state.

I made up my mind that I wouldn't dwell on it, that it sounded like relationship jitters. I would attempt to reach out to him again Monday. It was only Friday and that gave him plenty of time to think things through.

Ironically, I received a text from him Monday morning, before I had a chance to send one to him. He apologized for the previous text and confided in me that he had been struggling with multiple personalities since he was a child.

Never one to judge, I met him with kindness and understanding. To be perfectly honest, I was intrigued and wanted to know more. Because of my many years in therapy, psychology had become an interest of mine.

Our relationship progressed over the next several weeks but I had to admit that it was rather challenging. He would go through periods of communicating regularly and then not communicating at all. It was also difficult when he would have an episode. He would state facts about himself that I would later find out weren't really true. It was a difficult relationship to be in, but I couldn't give up on him.

I knew most people wouldn't even try to comprehend what he must be going through. *I can't give up on someone else the way everyone else has given up on me.*

Plus, being with a person with a different problem seemed safe. I theorized that someone with that kind of illness is used to being judged, so he probably won't judge me for having depression and anxiety. Then things took a turn for the worse when I considered suicide again. Stupidly, I confided in him how depressed I was feeling and admitted that I was considering suicide.

After only a few minutes, the response I received from him via text was: "Stay away from me you damn psycho."

I was absolutely blown away and had no idea how to even process his harsh words. I understood that his words were no doubt a product of his mental state but it didn't make me feel any better. All I had been looking for was someone to be there with me through the agony. Instead, family, friends of family, supposed friends of my own, neighbors, even mental health professionals, all didn't want anything to do with me because of my severe depression. I hated that I didn't matter enough to one single person for them to come to my aid.

People wouldn't abandon me if I wasn't severely depressed but how can I not be severely depressed if no one ever cares enough about me to not abandon me? What a horrific cycle! Not one single person will spend holidays or birthdays with me for more than an hour, leaving me to face the rest of the day completely alone. Doesn't anyone realize that what I really need as a gift for any one of those occasions is real family? Real family doesn't leave you

alone on holidays and birthdays. Why don't I matter enough to anyone to
not be alone when it matters most?

I grew increasingly frustrated. When I left my parents, I had arrived at
the point where I had finally seen that I did possess value.

Why can't anyone else see that I have value? Father doesn't see it, neither
does Mother, otherwise she wouldn't allow him to hurt me. Their friends
don't see it, otherwise they would believe me.

I attended job interview after interview, yet received no job offers. Apparently they didn't want to deal with my service dog. I couldn't work
without her. I knew I needed a job in order to be able to sever ties with
the abusive family I was stuck with. I knew that if I couldn't find a place
that would hire me, I would forever be stuck in that situation. I had started
my job search over a year ago, to no avail. Not knowing what else to
do, I began ending interviews with the facts about my situation, letting
potential employers know that I was in an abusive relationship, and that I
could not escape it without my own income. Still, no one cared enough to
hire me.

Believing that I was stuck once again, I grabbed a giant bottle of pills and
took to the roads. To this day, I'm not sure why I started driving around
before taking the pills. Maybe I thought that being in my car would feel
similar to the escape I first felt when I got my license? Maybe I was trying
to buy myself time for something I wished would happen?

After several hours of driving around aimlessly, I chose to call my best
friend. I told her that I had called just to chat when in reality, I really just
wanted to hear a friendly voice who cared. I was afraid to admit to her that
I was feeling suicidal again, because I knew she would try to dissuade me.
I honestly didn't want her to convince me not to do it. She seemed to be
enjoying life, having gone to college and acquiring a decent paying job, able
to pay her own way and purchase the things she wanted. I was happy for
her and at the same time extremely jealous at her lack of misery and ability
to hold down a job.

Reminiscing with her about all of our silly memories and inside jokes over the years helped ease my pain for a few hours. I couldn't escape that dependency was my reality. I was dependent on my abusers and I hated myself for it. But what could I do unless someone finally hired me? I felt completely unsafe without my dog, who had a proven track record of protecting me, so not bringing her anywhere was not an option, especially after the amount of traumatic events I had previously endured each time I had left the house.

Later that night, I took my medications in the dark, intentionally pouring extra pills into my hand before putting them into my mouth and swallowing. Hoping not to wake up in the morning, I went to sleep. Unfortunately, groggy as ever, I woke up the next morning, as angry as I was disappointed.

As if I needed further proof that I can't do anything right. Attempt number two and still kicking...and screaming. Will this hell ever end?

Later that week, my close friend from my church group called to check up on me because I hadn't been attending lately. We chatted for a bit and she shared with me the positive things happening in the lives of the other members of the group. She mentioned that some of the things seemed too crazy to be a coincidence. I did have to agree with her that some of the things did sound like a crazy coincidence. I was sure to bluntly remind her that there is no God.

"There is," she said simply, leaving it at that. I found it odd and equally comforting that she didn't push anything on me. It was something I wasn't used to.

Although I believe her motive behind calling me had been to spread positivity and attempt to cause me to reach out to a higher power that she believed would help me, it didn't work. The fights between my parents and I were less frequent but still occurring via phone. They still possessed control over me due to my lack of employment. I was still stuck with them, unable to escape.

Over the next few days, I had to admit that it seemed too crazy that everyone from the church group seemed to have better lives, and every prayer they had prayed was seemingly answered. The more I thought about it, the more my belief changed. I saw now that God had been present in my friends' lives from the church group. *But if He exists, why isn't He present in mine?*

This supposed "God" had allowed me to continue living in an abusive environment, allowed my mother not to listen to me or even remember my trauma or her own, He had taken several of my friends when I barely had any, allowed everyone to discard me like a piece of dog shit, and left me with no one there any time I had needed it most. And, contrary to the belief of the church people, I had absolutely no blessings to count whatsoever.

What God would allow that and for so many miserable years?

That's when a thought struck me like when a lightning bolt strikes down even the mightiest tree.

There is a God. It's obvious from my friend's lives... Everyone says there is a purpose, but my agony has gone on for so long. Too long. Too long to be a coincidence... I understand now... There is a God. But he has abandoned me too... Because I really am nothing. I am worthless... So worthless that he took my friends, but not me... He won't take me because even He doesn't want me... That's how worthless I am...

So worthless that even God won't take me. I'm worthless even in God's eyes.

Although I had previously thought that I couldn't feel any lower, I discovered that day that I had been wrong. This was my new low point. I was too worthless for God's love and grace.

For the next several months, my life continued on in agony, as it always had. I decided that since God didn't want me, attempting suicide was pointless, as I obviously would not be accepted into Heaven.

Now that my friend Heather had heard the truth on the other end of the phone line, I knew it was safe to discuss the situation with her in its entirety. I was beyond ecstatic that someone finally, after so many long, agonizing years, actually believed me. Even better was the fact that she was trying to help me figure out a way to remove myself from the situation.

Father's unannounced pop-ins had resumed, bringing all the feelings of anxiety and feeling trapped back to the surface. I relayed this information to my friend and she suggested that I have my locks changed. Informing her that any money I spent would have to come from him, she and her husband volunteered to purchase locks and also come over and accomplish the task for me. I was able to get approval from the maintenance man and change the locks.

While it was nice hearing the maintenance man apologize for my unfortunate situation and not say that he didn't believe me, I knew it was only because he had never met my father. After all, once people met Father with his ability to feign empathy like a professional actor, they would never believe me again.

The day after my friends came over to change the locks, Father attempted another unannounced visit. When his key didn't work, he proceeded to ring the doorbell over and over, as well as knocking and shouting my name. His loud persistence almost sent me into a full blown anxiety attack and I almost didn't answer the door or my phone when he then began calling me nonstop.

Then it occurred to me that if I refused to answer, he would no doubt call the police. Then knowing him, he would smile pretty and offer the officer a very believable story about how I was supposedly suffering from "some severe depression, anxiety issues, and some autism," as he always claimed.

Why would any officer believe anyone that good at faking it, especially when the daughter in question is unemployed and heavily medicated on psychiatric medication? Oh yeah, BECAUSE the daughter in question is unemployed and heavily medicated.

Realizing that I didn't stand a chance against Father or the police, I knew I had no choice. I broke down and let him in the door, despite my immense discomfort with him. Father questioned why his key didn't work, and I offered the lie that everyone in the apartment had received new locks. He then offered to go out and have a duplicate key made while he was there and I knew I was stuck.

How can I say no?

Being completely financially dependent on him, I had no choice in the matter. Especially since I knew no police officer would believe my side of the story, even if it was true.

The last officer thought I was crazy when I mentioned "PTSD" and disbelieved me that the man had actually been the one driving during the wreck, even though the insurance company also knew the truth.

I later recounted this event, as well as the possibility of police being involved, to my friends who had changed my locks, and we all realized that simply changing the locks wouldn't work. Completely overwhelmed by the weight of being in the same situation I had always been in, I broke down and began crying. "I can't escape. Unless someone hires me, I'm stuck. Yeah, I'm getting sober, but I still have a lot of medications to wean off of. And with him being that convincing... It's hopeless."

Then, another thought occurred to me. "And he knows my car, so he'll know if I'm home, even if I were able to turn off the tracker. Even if I got a job and became financially independent, he will never let me go. Even if I were to move, addresses are public information. As long as I'm alive, he will always be able to find me. Even with a job, there's no way out. I really am trapped in this hell!"

It was evident by their silence that my friends didn't know how to respond to that. We all knew that was all too true but none of us had any idea what to do about it. With all of my parents' acquaintances believing them, it was a game of odds. The number of people who believed him far outweighed the number of people who believed me. And it didn't help that I had been too afraid to confide in Rose about the majority of the things that Father had put me through. My parents had at least forty friends, family, neighbors, and acquaintances. But I had only myself and my two friends. The odds were forty to three.

I had made it perfectly clear to anyone and everyone who questioned me that my intent was to sever all ties with Mother and Father. When I mentioned this to people who knew me, I was met with much criticism and, when I refused to change my mind, shunning. This was so detrimental to my healing process and although I knew this, I also knew that I would never change my mind. I knew the truth down to the core of my soul. Father refused to change and Mother refused to see the truth.

It was bad enough that family, friends of the family, and neighbors refused to believe me. But soon, even people who knew me were expressing their distaste at my intentions to end my toxic relationship with my parents. One of my newfound friends, whom I had met at the dog park, told me, "I don't think you should try to leave your parents. In my experience, your parents are the only ones who are ever really there for you."

Another friend, who I would later sever ties with as well, told me, "But they're your parents! If you leave them, I think they will really freak out!"

My response was, "I don't care. No one is worth sacrificing my mental health and sanity over."

"But they're your parents," she continued. "You can't leave your parents. Besides, they adopted you."

Another former friend told me, "You're parents are so nice. And I totally understand older people. They mean well and really care about you."

Someone else told me, "They're your parents and they really care about you. Besides, you were chosen, since you were adopted."

It was all the same. Their pleas for me to stay connected to my parents and my refusal to do so.

"No I wasn't chosen," I responded. "I was settled for. They never wanted me. If they did, they would listen to me when I try to establish boundaries and they would respect those boundaries rather than trying to tear them down. If I was chosen, they would have heard the many cries for help over decades of my life."

Although I wasn't used to having friends, and part of me hated the thought of losing more friends, the more sane part of me realized that anyone who refused to acknowledge my problem was part of it. I had grown healthy enough to realize that I would rather be lonely and alone than settle for lesser quality people whom I claimed were friends. I would end up losing them in the end anyway and losing a part of myself again too.

The silver lining of adhering to this philosophy was that another new-found friend of mine from the dog park was actually starting to realize that there was a lot of truth to what I had been telling everyone. Upon recounting some of the conversations between Father and I, my friend Rosanna realized that things weren't in my head, as Father had led many to believe.

Realizing how difficult healing was becoming for me as everyone scolded me and shunned me, Rosanna saw how hard I was fighting to become sober off of all the medications. After confiding in her about my previous suicide attempts, she even told me, "You can call me anytime you really need to talk, even if its in the middle of the night."

I was surprised when later on, I called her, and she actually answered my call at two in the morning. She stayed on the phone with me until I calmed down enough to alleviate my stress. What a breath of fresh air! I was so grateful to her for that.

Age 30

After that, I decided I would try to live my life the best I could. I kept attending interviews to no avail, holding out for a job offer, and continued my journey toward complete sobriety. The only thing honestly keeping me from suicide was the belief that I wasn't even worthy of God's love.

One day, I went to order takeout from a restaurant, where I encountered a man who I found attractive. I complimented him on his hair, then went about my day. I later encountered the man twice more, and during the third encounter, he told me his name was Frank and then he asked for my phone number.

"I'm flattered," I replied, "but I'm still trying to get my shit together and really don't want to be involved with anyone right now."

"I'm just looking for a friend," he said, as men always do.

Knowing that I was being offered a line, I was flattered but continued to turn him down. However, upon his persistence, I eventually gave in and we exchanged numbers. He and I began chatting, and our relationship progressed in no time. Before we knew it, and to both of our surprise, we became an item.

Deborah's mother contacted me to check in. She mentioned how it looked like things were looking up for me. I couldn't help but agree. It was great keeping in contact with my friends' parents after her passing. It was like having a piece of her still with me.

Later, I called my friend from the church group. I felt that I needed her advice. Still, I had no luck with my job search, although that wasn't surprising with a service dog. After informing her that I still had no luck with my job search, I said, "Frank thinks I should do food delivery apps."

"Why don't you?" she responded.

Always having been told that I couldn't do things, my reply was, "Do you think I can?"

By now, my friend was well aware of Father's constant manipulation of my brain.

"What's stopping you?" she questioned, attempting to get me to think for myself for once.

All I could do was pause, deep in thought, as no one had ever asked me a question like that before.

"I... I don't know." I finally admitted.

And with that powerful question, yet another part of my brain broke free of Father's psychological locks.

I decided to go for it and had been delivering food with delivery apps for the past several months. I was enjoying my newfound self-reliance immensely. For the first time in my entire life, I felt a sense of self-worth. I knew I was well on my way to paying all of my own bills and was ecstatic that I could buy extra things that were wants, not just needs.

Still trying to make the relationship with Father work, I kept him at a distance and only saw him occasionally. I made it clear that if he continued to mistreat me, I would remove him from my life. I also finally made sure to establish boundaries with him, something I had finally been able to remember from therapy once I had successfully weaned off of the medication that had been so heavily clouding my brain.

One night, I made plans to meet with Father at a restaurant, just he and I, like we had used to do regularly years ago. We did some chatting and catching up, and things were going well for once, until they weren't. Seeing my phone on the table, he took it upon himself to pick it up and enter my old passcode like he had done a million times before.

When the passcode didn't work, he asked me casually, "What's the passcode?"

"Why do you always want my passcode?" I questioned him, for the first time ever.

"Why do you always have to be so secretive?" he countered, an obvious attempt at misdirection.

"I'm not being secretive," I responded honestly. "I'm just trying to have some sense of independence."

"Come on," he pressured, feigning his usual look of concern. "I'm your Dad. I care about ya. Just gimme the passcode."

"No," I responded politely. "I prefer to maintain my independence."

Again, he continued to pressure me, and again, I refused to give in.

After several minutes, he realized I was serious. He knew he was losing me.

In a fit of frustration, he exclaimed, "Fine!" and violently slammed my phone down onto the table with a disgruntled look on his face.

"Dad!" I yelled, surprised that he hadn't broken my screen and believing that he had probably hoped it would break so he could offer to buy me a new one.

Damn. The song is right. He really is just a child with a temper. Never again.

I vowed then and there that, no matter what he did, I would never again allow him to control any aspect of my life. I knew I was about to face the biggest battle I had ever faced, I just didn't realize how intense and crazy the battle would become.

Still attempting to work things out with my parents, Frank agreed to meet them, so one day we went over to their house. I made sure to warn Frank about Father's seemingly nice behavior and about his hidden abusiveness and intrusiveness.

I introduced Frank to them, Father putting on his usual pretense. Father asked Frank many questions. What he did for a living, how old he was, about the teenage son he had. Then came the more intrusive questions: what his last name was, as well as his phone number and address. Frank decided not to heed my warning about giving out his information. Just like everyone else, he was skeptical about my claims about Father.

On the way home, I asked Frank, "Why did you give him your number and address?"

"I didn't want to be rude," Frank responded.

"You're going to regret that," I stated.

"Why?" asked Frank.

"Because he'll give it out to people freely." I replied.

"He doesn't seem like he would really do that," said Frank.

Am I making a mistake dating Frank? Why is it so hard for people to believe what they can't see?

About a month later, Frank, his son, and I went over to my parents' house for Thanksgiving.

Father had assumed that since Frank and he had a few things in common, it was safe for him to reveal his true colors around him that day, which he did by coldly interrupting me mid-sentence at the dinner table and barking at me to, "Just listen to what I have to say!"

That didn't sit well with Frank, who took immediate notice of the apparent fear on my face. He knew it wasn't right for Father to not allow me to even speak my point of view or desires.

On the way home, Frank admitted to me, "I can see now how you could've had many issues with your father."

At another gathering with my parents, Frank leaned back in his chair in obvious discomfort as he heard Father's conversation.

Noticing this, I leaned in and asked, "You okay, babe?"

He responded, "Your father's so fake, it's disgusting." I was ecstatic.

At last, after all these years, someone else finally sees the truth! Finally, someone who's not jaded.

Hell bent on my independence, I had finally obtained a job with Frank at the restaurant and began working sixteen hours a day, six days a week so that I could sever ties as soon as possible. As one can imagine, working an abundance of hours left little time for much else.

One day, Mother sent me a big, long text with a bunch of updates as to what was going on in her and Father's life. I opened the text, but due to the length of it, didn't have time to read it. When I arrived home, I was exhausted after such a long workday. The next day, I received another text from Mother. It read:

"Ok, here we are 24 hours later and you STILL haven't answered me. Why don't you just clear the air and tell me what you think I did."

Instantly, anxiety flooded my body at the apparent illness of Mother, who was now clearly exhibiting delusions. The worst part was that she was acting as if she thought *I* was the one having the delusions. There was no doubt in my mind that Father manipulated her into thinking that I was avoiding her and that he probably wanted everyone they knew to think I was mentally ill.

After all, he can tell I'm trying to sever ties and that he's losing me for good. People might find out the truth unless he tells more lies.

Then, a thought occurred to me regarding Mother's text. I looked at the time she had sent the long text the previous day. It literally had been exactly twenty-four hours...to...the...minute. That's when I realized that she had probably been watching the clock, counting down to when it would be an entire day later, so she could grill me.

That was when I realized that Mother was well on her way to thinking just like Father wanted her to. An intensive sadness flooded my heart at Mother's quickly deteriorating mental state. I wished there was something I could do to save her but I knew my efforts would be futile. It had left me beyond exhausted and I had long been fed up with sacrificing my own health, both mental and physical, to try to save her. I showed Frank the text.

"Oh-kay..." was his response, along with an alarmed facial expression, to Mother's obvious neuroticism.

"This is why I'm done with them," I told him. "This is what Father does. She wasn't like this when I was a kid." Sadly, that was to only be the first time Father's actions put a strain on my relationship with Frank.

Now noticing a pattern of manipulation with every past relationship I had had, including friendships, I was scared.

Father's favorite hobby is driving a wedge between me and anyone I ever spend time with. It's like he's trying to scare everyone off. He wants to isolate me from everyone else so that I have no one to turn to but him.

I had successfully weaned off all except one of my medications but had accepted that I would always need it because the psychiatrist had told me so. Unfortunately, writing me a refill had somehow fallen through the cracks and the practice allowed me to run out.

The entire week that I was without my medication, I had immense rage, which caused me to yell at Frank uncontrollably for a week. At the end of that week as I was once again yelling at him, I stopped mid-sentence, finally realizing that I had been raging at him. To my horror, the withdrawal my body was having from the lack of medication had made it so that I had been literally completely unaware of my own actions.

Overcome with guilt after realizing what I had done, I couldn't take it anymore.

I turned to Frank, who was glaring at me angrily, "Oh my God!"

I paused, terrified as realization finally set in, and said again even louder, "Oh my God!"

Confused but still angry, Frank said shortly, "What?"

"I...I've been yelling...and for a week!" I exclaimed in shock, finally aware of what had transpired.

"Yeah..." Frank stared at me, dumbfounded, as he started to realize what was happening.

"I have to go." I said. "I'm not good for anybody," I then turned and immediately left Frank's apartment.

I got in my car and started driving. I wasn't sure where I was going but I wasn't going back to Frank and his son, who I had come to call my son as well. They didn't deserve to have to put up with that rage. At that moment, I hated myself more than I ever had before. I realized finally that I had reminded Frank's son of the sick mother that raised him and her abusive boyfriend. I grew sick to my stomach, thinking that I could never live with myself again.

Maybe I should kill myself. I can't live with what I've done. I didn't mean to but the medication made it happen and I can never erase the memory. Even if the agony I caused eventually leaves, the memory will always be there.

I was refusing Frank's many phone calls, his feable attempt to get me to come back. My guilt and immense self-hatred at what I had accidentally done pushing me to keep going. But Frank pursued me as I drove anyway.

I stopped at a gas station and fueled up my car. I had made up my mind to drive to Ohio.

I have to get as far away from them as possible so I'm not tempted to take him back and put them through that ever again. I'll have to find a new job there...

To this day, I don't know why I thought about Ohio or why I stopped when I saw Frank pursuing me in his car. Maybe it was the frantic look on his face, like he didn't want to lose me. The look on his face reminded me of how Mother had looked when I had threatened to slit my throat in front of them. I think Frank wondered if I was considering suicide again.

It was as if some other force had possessed my body. I stopped my vehicle along the exit ramp of the highway so Frank could catch up. When Frank pulled up behind me, we both exited our vehicles. Again feeling like some other force was controlling my body and met with an embrace. He convinced me to come back to his apartment with him. I knew I wouldn't be mistreated there and was beginning to feel that this was my new safe place.

I then called the psychiatrist's office in an attempt to obtain a refill. "Prescriptions are by appointment only," said the receptionist coldly. I already knew that but the company had not done their job like they had stated they would.

"I know," I emphasized calmly, "But I need it now."

"Ma'am, don't yell at me!" she responded.

Completely taken aback, I paused confused before responding, "I'm not yelling."

"When people yell at us, we're instructed to hang up on you," announced the receptionist coldly.

Then I heard a click and the line went dead.

What the fuck! Even the people who are supposedly "helping you" treat us like addicts. I wouldn't be an addict if your people hadn't prescribed me medications, you dumb ass! I didn't want these medications, but trusted you as well as previous practices that I "need the medications" in order to function properly. No wonder the stigma is so bad surrounding addiction and mental health. The practices are a major part of the problem!

Luckily, I was able to obtain the script my body needed from my general practitioner, who I had built an excellent rapport with during the last several years.

I was beyond appalled when another mental health professional later informed me that "you're lucky you didn't die" from that withdrawal.

What the fuck! That stupid practice was going to let me die?!

I thought I was doing a favor to everyone who might use that practice when I reported what had happened to an acquaintance of mine who worked in the mental health department of the local police department.

After recounting the events to him, he responded with, "Yeah, unfortunately that happens all the time."

I couldn't believe it. All those years of being led to believe that mental health practitioners were experts in that field in order to help people and that they created medications for a reason was clearly not the whole story at all, but rather, far from it. I was appalled by the whole industry. I had already endured a slew of "unlikely" side effects, and now I could've suddenly died? And after I had been told by several practitioners that it can be habit forming but the chances of developing an addiction are very slim. Yeah, slim for who?

After that, I began researching things and discovered several other people who had decided to come out about their stories with similar negative outcomes due to medication. Then I started researching what chemicals some companies put in the medications. That was when I swore off anything unnatural for life and vowed to never put anything man-made in my body ever again, at least as much as I could help it.

Why do so many people not realize how unsafe these medications are? Why is any of this not common knowledge? Why are the potential side effects made to seem less serious than they are for so many people? Someone should do something about this!

This was a very pivotal moment in my life that would later impact my career choice in a gigantic way. Months later, my sleep was a huge issue, or lack thereof. Diagnosed with insomnia, my doctor had prescribed a sleeping pill. It helped at first but would later prove to be ineffective. I had only slept for an hour and a half per night for the last three days, making it impossible for me to do my job.

I went to the stress center in the hospital, hoping that my lack of sleep had something to do with my mental state. After they asked me questions, they gave me the all clear, saying that I was fine mentally, my sleep must be insomnia.

After three days of no sleep, I received a text from my grandma. It was a meme that said, "When life gets tough, keep going."

I knew instantly that Father was at his abusive mind games again, making it his constant mission to discredit me. He had apparently shared with the family that my lack of sleep was due to a depressive episode, despite the fact that I had been denied entry to the hospital due to a sound mental state.

Later that day, Father gave me the number of a neighbor he had met, telling me that she could help with my depression. So it wasn't just family he was discrediting me to, nice! He kept insisting that I give the woman a call, as if he were trying to make me believe that I was ill, like he had done countless times before.

I refused, and let family and friends know that I had found out that my body had built up immunity to the sleeping pill. Nevertheless, people still questioned everything I did. Anyone who was associated with Father continued to take his words at face value.

Mother called me one day as they were preparing to downsize into a smaller house. She had called to share her shock with me, telling me that their realtor had noted a musty smell in the house and that she had recommended that they call some mold inspectors out to assess the situation.

Mother recalled incredulously, "The mold inspectors found five spots of mold in our house!"

I was in such awe at her disillusionment that I couldn't even respond.

Did she really not remember the many pleas from myself, the psychiatrist, the therapist, and the pulmonologist, who had each specifically told her that there must have been a reason, something in that house, that had made my lungs that severely inflamed?!! That was yet another clear and immensely painful sign of Mother's deteriorating mental state.

Father knew that he was losing control of me, and it was evident that he couldn't stand it. One day out of the blue, he called and told me that Frank and his son and I needed to be at their house around eleven in the morning "to help them move."

"Sorry, but we can't," I replied. "We have to work tomorrow."

Fed up with his attempts at control, and realizing that he wasn't going to stop, I hung up.

Then Mother called, reiterating what Father had just said.

After telling her we had to work, she said, "You're off Sunday, right?"

"Yeah," I replied, "but I can't take my only day off, my only day to catch up on sleep, to do physical work. I work sixteen hours a day in a physical job and my body needs the rest. I'm sorry, but we can't."

"Well we will close on the house in a week!" Mother implored. "We have to get everything out of there!"

I realized that Father intentionally waited until the last minute to let me know and that he deliberately put me in a spot that I couldn't get out of to prove to Mother that I was being selfish. And it worked.

Mother paused, then continued, "Well why don't you guys call off work then?"

I was assuming that Father put her up to that ridiculous comment but given the latest evidence of her mental state, I couldn't be sure.

"Are you serious?" I questioned. "That's not professional. This is just a stepping stone job, I get it, but I won't be eligible for a better one later on if word gets around that I called off work on a whim, for any reason! Besides, I'm living paycheck to paycheck, so it's not like I can afford to miss work anyway."

Knowing that Father would offer me money in order to help me out, I flat out refused. I didn't want him to have anything more to hang over my head, as he often did.

"I'm putting up boundaries like my therapist told me," I said. "I'm sorry if Dad doesn't like it but I'm done being pushed around. Goodbye."

With that, I hung up the phone.

The phone calls were exhausting and I was beginning to feel more than a little harassed. My parents were making it really hard to stay on track with my sobriety. I felt that Father knew this and was intentionally trying to wreck things.

Once I'm out of his life, everyone will suspect that there really was a problem, and he knows that. That's why he's seeking to keep control.

After recounting these events to Frank, I told him that Father was intentionally dragging my name through the mud as usual.

"If these people think they know you so well, shouldn't they figure out that there has to be more to the story?" asked Frank.

"You would think," I replied. "You would think after all those years that they would know me better than that. Yet somehow, no one can figure out he's full of shit."

The next day, I received a text from their friend, asking, "Why are you refusing to help your parents move?"

Wow. Does anyone know me at all? What's wrong with these people that they all believe I'm such a piece of shit?

I responded with, "I'm not. Like I told them, I have to work."

Her response was: "You can make time to help them move."

I decided I wouldn't dignify her accusations with a response. I finally realized that I deserved so much better. Knowing that any response was both futile and a complete waste of my time, I blocked her number right then and there.

When I called my friend from the church group, proud of what I had done, she said exactly what I had already been thinking, "You don't deserve to have to put up with that harassment."

I was extremely grateful for my friend's involvement in my life at that moment. It was clear that my time with her had paid off. Finally, I was able to think on my own.

Father wouldn't quit his gaslighting, however. Days later, he posted a picture of their friends' son on Facebook, saying, "When your own daughter won't help you move, you appreciate help from the children of friends who actually do care enough to help."

I rolled my eyes, realizing that he was attempting to guilt me in order to gain a rise out of me. *It's not gonna work, motherfucker! Not anymore!* Then I chuckled to myself, finding his attempt pathetic as well as completely childish.

Later, after Father and Mother had moved, it had rained, causing more mold in their old house. Since the new owners hadn't taken possession yet, Father returned back to the old house to spray more mold remover on the moldy spots.

I was appalled that he would knowingly hide mold from somebody just to get more money.

Since I was on the phone with him at the time, I asked, "There's still mold in the house?! What about the new people?"

"Once it's outta my hands, it's theirs now!" he responded icily.

Wondering why he was sharing this heartless action with me, I proceeded to ask, "But what if they get sick?"

"That's their problem," he said.

I felt sick to my stomach even knowing this information, even sicker realizing that this heartless asshole was supposedly my father. That night, I couldn't stop thinking about how sick that house had made me and how

Father had never even cared that I couldn't breathe. I just prayed the new owners would take action before they got as sick as I did.

One day at work, my boss asked me to go and pick up a some sodas. On the way back to the restaurant, the lid on one of the drinks popped off, spilling into the charging port of my car. That was a huge problem. I needed to be able to charge my phone while driving, otherwise I would have no way to use GPS.

Unfortunately, the only repair shop that would fix the issue was about a half hour away, near Mother and Father's house.

I later received a random call from Father, during which he let me know that he had been driving by and had seen my car in the parking lot of the repair shop. He had taken the liberty of paying for the repairs "as a gift from me since you've been working so hard."

I refused to thank him because I realized that the only reason he had done it was because he realized that I was becoming independent. He wanted something to hang over my head, as usual, and knew that paying for the car repairs would, no doubt, make me feel obligated.

When I recounted this to my therapist, my anger was evident at Father's seemingly kind gesture, realizing the strings that were attached to that act of kindness.

"He only did that to make me feel obligated to keep him around," I said in disgust, overwhelmed by feelings of entrapment.

My therapist responded simply with, "Well don't let it."

That comment stunned me as I literally leaned back in the chair.

Having insinuated to me for so long what to think, do, and feel, I could only pause, deep in thought.

Oh my gosh!" I stammered, "You're right. I have a choice in the matter."

The Downfall, The Aftermath, The Refusal

Age 31

Things between Frank and I progressed so well that we decided to take a big leap. I moved all my things into a storage unit and then moved in with him and our son. Not really having anyone else at the time, Father and Mother of course offered to help us move into the storage unit.

Later, Father tried yet another ploy for control that would have undoubtedly led to more social isolation if I had given in as I would've years before. "Just in case something happens," he said, "or in case things don't work out with you and Frank, you really should give us the code to your storage unit and also make us a copy of the key to Frank's apartment."

Of course, realizing that this was nothing more than a ploy, I adamantly refused, leaving Father to grow increasingly more frustrated.

Inviting my parents to the birthday party that one of my bosses so graciously decided to throw me was my last-ditch effort to maintain a relationship with them.

When Frank and I arrived, I noticed that Father's vehicle was parked in the handicapped spot near my bosses house.

"Why is he parked there?" I thought aloud in front of Frank. "The guest parking lot is at the end of the street."

When I saw Father, I informed him, "You can't park there."

Not even caring enough to learn my boss' name, he replied, "The girl said I could."

Suspecting foul play as usual, I then proceeded to question my boss, "My dad said you told him he could park there?"

"Yeah," she responded, "He said he had a bad back."

Without a handicap placard, his illegal parking could have been reported to my boss' rental agency, which in turn could have put my job in jeopardy.

What the hell is wrong with him?! This is the only job I've been able to get and after having searched for any job at all for over two years! He would probably be glad if I lost my job then I would have no income other than the money he would no doubt try to offer me. Cold-hearted, lying bastard!

For years, I had struggled with my name. Hearing it brought me much pain. Every time I heard it all I heard was Father's harsh ridicule. Father having always said, "God damnit, Eliza!" made the name Eliza feel like my last name, with my first being God, and my middle being damnit. Hearing someone say my name had become extremely difficult. It was a painful reminder that I was apparently a God damn person, whom even God couldn't love.

So I told Frank that I didn't care what he called me as long as he didn't call me Eliza. I told him I'd rather be called shit head than that!

After much thought, Frank came up with a name suggestion, sort of as a nickname for me. Amber. For the next several months, I went exclusively by Amber. Several months later, however, out of the blue, he called me Tambryn as a joke. I liked it.

A few months later, I decided that I wanted to adopt Frank's son. We were getting so close and I wanted his son to have a mother figure in his life so he knew how much he was loved. I felt mentally strong enough to take on such responsibility and that he was mine at this point anyway. I told Frank this and that I wanted to pay half of our son's needs each month.

Frank said he appreciated the thought but that I should just take care of myself, and not worry about any other expenses. He realized that doing so would throw me into a completely different tax bracket, causing me to lose my health insurance.

We went around and around about this matter for a week, constantly at an impasse. Being told what to do, or, in this case, what not to do, reminded me too much of Father's control. So I put my foot down.

"I've always been dependent on others financially," I told Frank, "and I've always hated myself for it. I finally figured out that I *can* work, and that I *can* pay my own way in life."

I was nervous. I realized this could cause a huge riff in our relationship and could potentially lead to a breakup between Frank and I. Yet after so many years of extremely painful existence as well as complete lack of control to do anything that I wanted to do, I chose to say it anyway, despite what might happen. I was, finally, and also quite proudly, refusing to settle.

After a slight hesitation, I dared to say it, "Sorry, but this is a deal breaker. I can't be with somebody who won't let me be independent."

Realizing how important this matter was to me, Frank immediately put his hands up in a surrendering manner, saying, "Alright. I still don't agree with your decision but if it's *that* important to you, I will respect your decision."

Several weeks later, Mother texted me asking for gift ideas for myself as well as for Frank and our son.

I responded with, "Thanks for thinking of us but don't worry about gifts for us this year. I can't afford to buy gifts for anyone except my immediate family."

Instantly, Father called, saying, "You can't show up with gifts for just us."

"I said immediate family," I responded. "Immediate family is who you live with."

"You *can't* show up to Christmas without gifts," he voiced.

"I can't afford gifts and the only people who will care if I bring any are you and Mom," I countered.

"Well, why can't you afford gifts?" he pried. "Mom and I are *giving* you money every month, which should cover all your expenses. And now that you're working, that should cover anything else."

"If you must know," I responded snidely, clearly annoyed that I still had little privacy even though I had moved out of their house, "I've decided to adopt Frank's son."

"*What!*" he yelled furiously. "Frank is taking advantage of you! He shouldn't be *making* you do that!"

Wow. Is this how he brainwashes Mother? Why does he think that would even work on me now that I'm clearly healthy?

"He's not," I replied. "It was my idea and it's my decision."

"Frank is taking advantage of you! He shouldn't be *making* you do that!" he said again.

"Again," I stated, "It's *my* decision."

"Frank is *taking advantage* of you!" It was apparent that Father was desperately attempting to foist this false belief onto me. "He shouldn't be *making* you do that!"

"It's my life, not yours," I responded. "I'm done taking orders from you."

"Here," Father attempted, "Mom and I will just *give* you money."

"No you won't," I countered.

"Yes we will," Father argued. "Mom and I will each put an extra $400 in your account, so you can get gifts for everybody."

Father was desperately searching for a string to dangle over my head, as usual. This time, I realized this, and that I actually had a choice. This time, I wasn't giving in. This time, I wouldn't give it to him.

"No, you won't," I stated strongly. "Every time you do that, I feel like a piece of shit." Right after I said that last part, I regretted it, realizing that I shouldn't have admitted any weakness to someone so uncaring who would no doubt use that to his advantage.

"We're *giving* you the money," Father said.

"If you do," I responded, "I won't show up to Christmas at all."

"Just take the money," Father begged.

"Nope." I said finally.

With that, I disconnected the phone line.

I thought back to Father's repetitive words. It seemed like he was used to repeating himself but he hadn't done that with me before. *Is that how he brainwashed Mother so easily? Did he just repeat phrases over and over again for hours and days until she believed them?*

I noticed that he had emphasized "give" each time he said it, an indicator that he was attempting to make me feel obligated again. No sooner had I hung up, then Mother called me.

"Hello?" I answered.

"Frank is *taking advantage* of you!" she shouted. "He shouldn't be *making you* pay his son's bills!"

"I've decided to adopt him," I stated, thinking that Father probably had neglected to tell her that information.

"That's not *your* son!" Mother shouted frantically. "That's not *your* responsibility!"

I didn't appreciate her referring to my son as a "that," instead of a "he," and realized that Father was no doubt trying, through Mother, to get me to disassociate from Frank and my newfound son.

I responded, "That's *my* decision."

"Frank is *taking advantage* of you!" she almost sounded like she was begging me to believe that, just as she clearly did.

A wave of deep sadness and grief flooded over me as I realized how much more ill Mother had so quickly become since I hadn't been around. *I warned her. Repeatedly, for years, I warned her*, I reminded myself, now working to remove the doubt that Father had so diligently spent years embedding into my brain.

"No, he's not," I responded. "I wouldn't allow anyone to take advantage of me anymore."

"That's not *your* son," Mother repeated, her voice still elevated. "That's not *your* responsibility! He shouldn't be making you—"

"I had to threaten to break up with him to get him to go along with it," I shouted back, now fed up more than ever at Mother's lack of ability to think for herself.

Sounding like a broken record yet another time, Mother shouted, "That's not *your* son!"

"Okay," I countered, "then by that logic, I'm not *your* daughter!"

Running through my mind was the metaphorical "Ooooh," that so often plays after a statement calling a character out in a sitcom when that character is out of line.

I truly believed that she would pause, feeling slighted, but would then realize the error in her judgement.

But instead, she didn't hesitate as she responded with, "That's different. We paid a lot of money for you!"

Wow... Wow... She's getting really far gone. She would've realized her error a year ago.

Later, I was horrified to discover that Father had transferred the money into my account regardless, seemingly in spite of my defiance. I decided that, not only was I not going to buy gifts, I was also boycotting the family Christmas gathering.

Not that anyone would figure out what was really going on. God knows Father will make up some believable story about why I supposedly can't be there.

Desperate to put a stop to Father's easy access to manipulation, I went to the bank and the cellular store, where I attempted to remove Father from the accounts.

At both places, I was disappointed to hear, "We can't do that without your father here."

"But he's abusing me," I countered.

Still, I was told shortly and awkwardly that there was nothing they could do, each party turning and leaving at such an awkward conversation they clearly didn't want to be in the middle of.

It was then that I considered applying for a protective order against Father. Upon researching what that would entail, I realized that that would not work either, as both parties, myself and my parents, would have to be present. Father would undoubtedly tell all of their friends that his "autistic, mentally ill" daughter is trying to pursue legal action against him, then they would all show up claiming that he is a really great father and that I am delusional. It would be my word against all of theirs and why would any one believe the person on a bunch of psychiatric meds whose parents are paying for some of their living expenses? Even though Heather and her husband knew the truth, it wouldn't be enough without proof.

I could get the paperwork from the abuse center with Father's name on the intake form but I don't think that would be enough to stop them all in convincing the judge that this is all in my head. If only I could prove that he is lying to them all and that Mother and I were brainwashed. But if they can't see that Mother is ill, then they definitely won't see that I'm not.

It was clear after several texts and calls to Deborah's mother over the last several months that Father had polluted my good name with his lies. He had no doubt convinced them of my supposed autism and mental illness, evident by the fact that she was no longer responding to my texts or calls.

Great! God already took Deborah. Now Father took her family from me. At least they gave me some of her things before they abandoned me, too.

Realizing how hard the abandonment was becoming for me, Rosanna sent me a text out of the blue, "I saw this and thought this might help you feel better about things."

It was a photo from a book, with an excerpt explaining that when people are considering cutting ties with family members, people often respond with judgment and hatred, making it an imprisoning guilt trip. It mentioned to ignore people who are judging you for wanting to end the relationship and that there are usually good reasons as to why someone would even consider doing so with family. It went on to say that someone is not a bad person for choosing to remove themselves and that each person has every right to preserve their integrity and overall health by removing themselves from toxicity or abuse.

Thoroughly fed up with the abuse, I followed the suggestion of my therapist and texted my parents a long message, explaining to them that they had damaged me significantly and that I was doing better now that I had not been exposed to Father's harsh ridicule. I chose to call him out on his abusive ways and I bared my soul within that message.

The message read:

"Why is everyone texting me when I've politely asked for space? I feel healthier than I have ever been, but there is still something holding me back. Having major depressive disorder is never easy, but the comments I heard at "home" made it worse. In the midst of a severe anxiety attack or depression, I heard, 'God damn it, Eliza. Don't start that shit again.' Whenever I said I couldn't help it, I heard, 'Just get off your ass and do something, that would help. Do anything other than lay around like some lazy slug.' I always felt like nothing I ever did was ever good enough. When I said that once, it was 'What do you want, a medal?' Because of that it was obvious to me that I was inadequate as a human being, so why even try? Everyone I met thought less of me. I went through countless 'friends' who left and dated several guys who weren't nice. At the time, I didn't care. At least that way I had someone who pretended to understand me, instead of being completely alone. After all, holidays I had no one around because you guys went to parties or wouldn't stay with me, despite my telling you that I needed someone, anyone. Things changed when I met some neighbors at my apartment complex. They confided in me, and I in them. One night, my depression got so bad and I was so suicidal that I felt I couldn't go on. I figured that they wouldn't understand, but didn't know anyone else at the time, so I called them and told them how I was feeling. They said they'd come right over, and I expected that they wouldn't really. They did, however, and held me while I cried, and told me how awful they felt watching me in such pain. That was a strange feeling. No criticisms, nothing about how it was MY fault that I felt that way. From that point on, I realized that my life *has* value, and that it had all along. I feel healthier now than I have ever been, but I still struggle remembering my childhood home life that was so painful. In order to keep myself healthy, I've taken a better job, have made new friends, and have lots of people who actually are there for me, more than just financially. I'm sorry if this makes you mad, but I don't like who I become around you. It brings me great pain and all those feelings of being insecure, inadequate, alone, and angry come flooding back when I see you. My therapist, my friends and I all agree that it's best if you leave me alone now. The pain is too much and it's been affecting me at my new job when the memories arise. I'm making a new life for myself, with a better job, better friends, and people who give me emotional support. Please let me be and don't contact me."

The next day, I received a phone call from another one of their friends. I ignored it, but she left a voicemail:

"Hi Eliza! It's Katie. I was just calling to chat and find out how delivering food is going. Give me a call back and we can chat. Talk to you later, bye."

Seriously?! I bear my soul to them exposing my raw feelings and Father's still at it, using his friends to continue to harass me?! Do they think I'm stupid? Does Father actually think I won't realize that she will report back to them? Why can't he leave me alone? And why can't all their friends realize that they're just spies? They're never going to fucking leave me alone! This will never end!

Weeks later, a brilliant idea occurred to me and I marched down to my local courthouse, where I took a different kind of legal action against Father. I decided to petition for a legal name change and go into hiding so that no one else would have to be involved in the court hearing. That way, Father would no longer be able to maintain control over me. No one would be able to look up my address since they wouldn't know my name. That would put an end to the harassment from their friends and to Father showing up out of the blue.

After explaining my situation to the clerk, she explained that petitioning for a legal name change alone would not do the trick. It's a requirement that name changes be public record. She informed me that since I was in an abusive situation, I would have to request a court hearing in order to have the record of my name change sealed. That way, it would be hidden from the public and no one would be able to look up the information about my name change.

I guess it's worth a try. Not that anyone will believe me. The last judge didn't. Maybe Heather will actually step up for me, unlike anyone else has, and appear in court.

After filling out the forms, the receptionist said that I would be given a court date via phone call, during which time I could present my case to one of the judges. All that was left was to pay the hefty filing fee, which I paid for with the money that Father had given me demanding that I buy Christmas gifts for people.

The perfect middle finger to the bastard!

I was extremely nervous about going to court again, since the last judge I sat in front of had insinuated that I was a no good freeloader, and basically called me lazy to boot. I called Heather and asked if she would go with me to court, expecting in the back of my mind to be abandoned yet again. I realized it was a really big thing to ask but knew that if I didn't, I would never be free of Father's control and abuse. To my surprise, she didn't even hesitate to agree to be there and even suggested I bring evidence from my medical file and contact my therapist regarding the situation as well.

I knew she was right, I already had so much on Father: my medical file stating that I am mentally sound and soon-to-be released from therapy, as well as the lack of autism disorder present on the list of issues I had been suffering from, my file from the abuse organization listing Father's name as my abuser, as well as she, her husband, and my boyfriend as witnesses. Nevertheless, these facts didn't stop me from feeling extremely nervous.

The worst part was knowing that I couldn't discuss this process with anyone other than Frank and our son, Heather and her husband, Rose, Rosanna, and of course, my therapist. I realized that it was too risky to involve anyone else that I thought I could trust. I had already been disappointed so many times before, believing that people would question my side of the story.

The next several months were quite difficult. I knew that I would no longer be able to speak to anyone from my former life if the name change was approved. In addition to severing ties with Mother and Father, and all of their associates, I also had to stop communicating with my few other friends from childhood. That was hard. I had grown up with these people. But I couldn't take any chances on letting anyone in on what was about to happen. I couldn't risk someone reporting it back to Father. At this point, I had no idea who I could really trust other than the aforementioned people.

The day of the hearing, I was an emotional wreck. In the back of my mind I really didn't think that my luck would change and expected to continue being stuck in misery for the rest of my life.

Countless family members never believed me, their friends never believed me, most neighbors never believed me, the social security judge didn't believe me and the policeman hadn't believed me during the wreck. Why would things be any different this time?

The judge entered the courtroom and introduced himself, then looked at us and asked, "Is it okay if our stenographer records this?"

"Yeah," Heather responded. All I could do was nod nervously.

Sitting there in front of the judge terrified me, almost more than dealing with Father, even with my trusted friend alongside me.

Too afraid to speak, my friend, Heather, began for me.

"I'm just here for moral support," she told him.

"I see," responded the judge. "Why are we here today?"

Still unsure of everything, I looked at Heather for reassurance.

"It's ok," she said. "Tell him why we're here."

Quietly and unsurely, I finally said, "I'm in an abusive situation."

Afraid to go into more detail, I simply offered, "I have proof in my medical file and also I have this letter here from my therapist."

"Okay. Instead of having someone come and bring the evidence, the way it works in this type of court setting is we have you read the information out loud to the court."

The shakiness in my voice indicated my fear to both the judge and Heather.

In short, the note stated that the issues I had been having most of my life were a result of a lack of support at home starting from a young age and that Father had led me to believe that no one loved me and that I was incapable of doing anything without his guidance or say so. The information stated that I previously could not think on my own.

After I finished presenting the evidence, the judge gave the final decree saying I was granted my complete legal name change. I would no longer be the scornful, pathetic "God damnit Eliza," but rather, Tambryn Crimson, the free bird phoenix who would emerge from the flames of hell and be resurrected from having been nothing but forgotten, insignificant ashes.

The sound of the judge's gavel clanging against the podium resembled a coffin lid slamming, sealing Father's evil crypt.

For a change, *I* was the one who was in sheer disbelief. I had actually been granted the ability to hide from Father so I could begin healing without him sending anyone to unknowingly stalk and harass me.

I had no idea how I would react or even how I thought I would react. I was dumbfounded by my new reality, which Heather quickly figured out.

"It's over!" she exclaimed. "It's finally over!"

I still had a zombified look on my face. I couldn't believe it was over. Heather began shaking me, attempting to help me grasp my new reality.

"It's done!" Heather continued.

Suddenly, her words sank in, and I began sobbing relentlessly, tears streaming down my face like a waterfall. Completely overjoyed, it honestly felt as if a plethora of literal weight had been lifted off of my tiny, weak shoulders. This was the first time I ever cried tears of joy rather than misery or sorrow.

"It's over!" Heather continued again as I still attempted to fully grasp my newfound freedom. "He *can't* hurt you anymore! That's it! That's the final nail in his coffin!"

Overcome with relief, I smiled the rest of the day, walking around still overcome with shock and joy.

I'm finally free!

Heather and I went back to the waiting room to ask the secretary when we should expect to be back for the final process of the case. The hearing we had just attended was intended to approve the need to have the case file sealed and hidden from public record. The initial paperwork I had filed stated that there would be a second hearing scheduled after the first one, to make the name change official.

The secretary went to ask this question to the court judge, who had already called the next appointment into the court room. Apparently, the judge must have been moved by my great emotional display of relief that he requested the person who had a hearing after mine step back outside. Heather and I were surprised to be invited back into the courtroom, where the judge asked me to swear an oath that I wasn't changing my name to evade creditors (questions which were the usual procedure for all name changes) and then placed his signature on the final document right then and there.

I was very moved that someone finally cared enough about me to go to such lengths to protect me, and a stranger at that!

With the sealed court order, I was then able to acquire my own bank account as well as my own phone line. Father no longer had access to my bank account and his minion of spies no longer had my phone number. Finally, I was able to start the healing process.

The entire process to change my name and go into hiding was quite lengthy, causing me to struggle for several more months. First, I had to obtain a new birth certificate, then a new social security card, then a new driver's license. Unfortunately, each of these things took about a month to obtain, forcing me to endure being "God Damnit Eliza!" a little longer.

After I obtained all of the necessary documents, I cockily marched back down to the phone store, with Frank by my side, and showed them the court order, where they finally gave me my own phone line.

Father and his minions won't have my number, or my name for that matter, and won't be able to contact me! I kept feeling this wave of relief at each new step.

Then it was on to the bank, where I opened my own account.

"Unfortunately," said the banker, "we can't remove any of the money from the account. We can reroute any incoming paychecks you get to the new account, but can't remove any money from this account without his permission, since he owns it. I'm sorry."

It was disappointing, but I understood, and honestly, didn't care. *I wasn't kidding any of the times when I said, "There is no money worth the abuse!"* I am proud to say that when I left the abuse, I left the money behind.

I could just hear Father's anger, realizing that he would undoubtedly react quite angrily when he received the notification from the bank regarding my having been removed from the account. I wished that I would have had the privilege of witnessing his reaction.

Within a week, Father had texted Frank. One of their many spies had discovered that my phone line was no longer in use.

"Hi Frank. Katie called and told me that Eliza's phone had been disconnected. What's going on?"

Frank responded that I had gotten my own phone line.

Father's text read, "She's wanting to distance herself from us, that I get. But, as with any child, no parent is perfect. Mistakes are made. Feelings are hurt. There is no handbook for parenting."

"That doesn't make any sense," Frank told me as he shared this information with me. "There are a lot of them." Then he added, "You were right. He did also try to get your info."

I had come to know Father's game quite well and had already warned Frank that this would happen.

Frank read the next portion of Father's text: "Please give me Eliza's new number so we have it in case something happens and I need to reach her."

Frank asked, "Why would he need your number? He has mine."

"Because this is what he does," I responded. "He's trying to get back his control of me. If he gets my number, he can have everyone harass me again and try to spy on me."

Frank sent the response, "She doesn't want to give out her number and I will respect her wishes."

Father responded with yet another brilliant example of his feigned empathy, "Take care of her and yourself. Her mother is so torn up."

Yeah, she is, but you can't even pretend that you care? You really never gave a single damn about me. "Her mother is tore up", not "we're" tore up. Sounds about right.

Heather and I both recognized that his last comment was an attempted guilt trip designed to make me want to reach out to Mother.

That asshole really won't release control! How pathetic. Give it up. You'll never get me back. As for Mother, I warned her countless times per day that this would happen. It's not my fault that she didn't heed the warning, or even remember it, knowing her.

Although the majority of the trauma was over, I later went on to find out from Frank more information that I would later have to work to process.

Apparently, when Frank first met Father, he had asked Frank for "help with something in the basement", as was Father's custom with anyone new I introduced he and Mother to. I had assumed that he was having the fatherly talk with him, as I assumed he had many times before, I found out otherwise.

Father had used his manipulative tactics and had told Frank, "I appreciate your interest in Eliza, but be prepared, she's a lot to deal with. She struggles with some severe depression and anxiety issues and some autism. Her mom and I really do try to care for her but she doesn't quite understand that. Good luck, I hope you can handle her. I'll give you a week. God bless you for trying."

No wonder everyone, friends, boyfriends, neighbors, all abandoned me. It was by Father's evil design! He knew that if he didn't try to scare people off, I would probably find someone who would get me away from him.

Almost a year later, I assumed that since Mother had been trapped with Father so long, it was time to enter into her life again. I thought that if I entered back into her life, she would see how much better my life was now that Father wasn't in it, and it would might give her the courage she needed to finally leave him.

Especially since she knows that I will not stay in her life if he is around. Why would she not leave him if it meant losing me? And she wouldn't choose him over me since I treat her well. Right?

I downloaded an anonymous texting app and reached out to her. I made it perfectly clear that "I'm only communicating with you now to show you that living without Paul can be done and how much healthier I am because of it." I also reiterated, as I had previously stated countless times before, that our relationship was only temporary unless he wasn't in the picture.

I took Mother out, without Father, and one occasion even treated her friends to lunch as well, hoping that they would see the difference in me and recognize that it was because Paul was no longer around. I even openly referred to him as "Paul," not Father.

No one seemed to notice, however, and having two identities, using my old name around Mother and her associates, and my new name around the safe, healthy people I associated with now, quickly wore on me. Living this double life had made my newfound, stress-free life complicated again, and honestly, it was too much for me. But realizing that Mother had felt abandoned, I just had to try one last time to save her.

One of my friends warned me, "I know you want to care for your mother but I hope you take my advice and stop talking to her, because the trauma will remind you of the painful memories whether you like it or not." That is some of the best advice I've ever received because it was so true.

I established strict boundaries with Mother. I constantly was reminding her that I was back communicating with her so she could see how healthy I am now that Paul isn't around. She reacted as if I were her mother, as if she were being disciplined, listening intently, afraid to do something wrong.

"But this is only temporary unless Paul is out of the picture," I continued, "because I can't go through being controlled again and having my boundaries disregarded. I will not be around if he still is. I will not keep someone in my life who makes me sick. And I will not be able to maintain respect for you if you continue to stay with him." It was all a futile attempt to get her to see she was being controlled too.

One day I asked her if she wanted me to come by. I had a few extra minutes before work and no surprise, she responded with, "Paul's outside, just so you are aware. I don't want to force you into a situation you're not ready for."

"What do you mean, not ready for?" I asked her. "I told you, I will never speak to him again. He's burnt that bridge and refuses to help rebuild it, so no, never again." I didn't go see her that day.

I was growing increasingly frustrated with Mother. She was still unwilling to see or even slightly open her eyes to the truth about her idolized husband. It quickly became clear that Mother was still too wrapped around his finger and that she had attempted to share with Paul details about my life, despite my request not to.

I could just imagine what he must have said to her, using his ever convincing look of fake empathy, "That's *my daughter*. I raised her. I should get to know how she's doing."

While talking to Mother on the phone, I suddenly heard Father's voice in the background, talking to his dog. The echo in his voice made it evident to me that she had me on speakerphone.

"Why am I on speakerphone?" I demanded angrily. She didn't respond.

"I made it perfectly clear that knowing how I am doing is a privilege and that Paul is no longer permitted that privilege!"

Maybe now I should tell her that a court judge has seen proof that he is abusive and that I am not even supposed to be involved with her at all. I'm sure she would change her tune then. I decided to leave that out.

"I made my boundaries perfectly clear." I continued. "Why would you allow someone in my life who abuses me? I told you that if you disrespected my boundaries, you would not be permitted in my life either. Why should I not stop communicating with you if you can't respect me the way I'm asking you to?"

Still, there was more silence on Mother's end of the line.

Reflecting on things now, I should have done just that and immediately removed her from my life for disrespecting the boundaries that I had so firmly established were a direct correlation to my health, which had never been good until Father was out of my life.

After that, our only conversations were about what she did that day. I knew it was unsafe to relay any personal information to her. She was clearly still so far gone and very much under his spell.

It was too painful to admit at the time, but I already feared that she was too far gone to ever see the light. So instead, I kept pursuing her, unwilling to give up the relationship I once had with her, even though on some level I already knew that the person she once was no longer existed. Because this was too much for me to acknowledge, I stuffed those logical thoughts down and chose to commit a very hurtful yet overlooked form of self-harm: denial.

I realized that the allotted time I had given her, five months, had passed, and she still, much to my dismay, was completely unwilling to leave her abuser or even acknowledge that that is what he truly was. Even worse, she had chosen to forget all of the painful memories I had reiterated to her over those months, as if the conversations I had previously had with her had never happened.

I realized it was time to tell her the truth. Although I wished that I could put the conversation off with it being close to Christmas time, I couldn't bear it any longer. It was time that she was faced with the painful, horrible truth of the reality that she had caused me to live in.

Maybe since it's Christmas time, it will hit her harder and that might be what she needs to realize the reality of her abusive situation.

She had asked me about a piece of mail that my aunt had tried to send to the address they had for me. It had been sent to my old legal name at the address they had for me, which we had since moved from. Mother knew we had been house hunting, but I had deliberately kept from her the fact that we had obtained a place and had actually moved as a part of my going into hiding, which it was now time to tell Mother about. I actually thought that when I told her, she would be in such shock that a judge ruled her husband abusive that she would finally leave him.

I responded to her text, letting her know that Paul hadn't even bothered to learn our correct address. I let her know that in order for me to be able to function and hold down a job, I had been referred to a place that specializes in abuse, and that the place had reiterated that my problems were all related to Paul and his abuse. I told her that since Father had refused to leave me alone, it had been preventing me from healing. I went on to tell her that I had taken the painful yet necessary action of going to court, where the court judge decreed that Paul was not safe to be around, and that he and anyone who knows him is not allowed to contact me or know where I am. I ended the message with, "I love you and hope that one day you realize that you don't deserve to be abused," even including a heart at the end.

She waited an entire week to respond. I have since deleted the text but still see the black letters in the white text bubble etched into my mind, years later:

"Well here we are a week later and I STILL can't believe my eyes. Are you sure this is what you want?"

SERIOUSLY?! You think I want this?! NO! This is far from what I want? This is my worst fear come to life, my worst nightmare a reality, my most important prayer forever unanswered. My world shattered. Satan has won.

You're exactly what he wanted you to become. And everything I prayed for years that you wouldn't.

"Congratulations on your new home, an answer to many prayers on your behalf."

I love the snide attitude. The humor's making me feel so much better. What about all the prayers I stayed up late obsessing about and praying on behalf of you? The prayers that were supposed to restore your blind sight, mental health, and sense of self worth.

"I guess all that's left to say is, Merry Christmas. My heart is broken."

You're lucky that your heart just now broke. You've been breaking mine for nearly twenty years and you never even felt it, even after I told you time after time, day after day, night after night. And you still can't see it! I tell you that your husband has officially been deemed unsafe by a federal court judge and this is how you react? Why can't you see the gravity of the situation?

My mind was completely blown as my entire sense of reality shattered right then and there. *How could she not even realize? How did she get so sick?*

That was the absolute worst day of my entire life, hands down. That was when I realized that my mother was too far gone to ever come back to me. That was when I realized she would never be able to be a part of my life ever again. That was when I realized that my mother was my father's 2.0. That was when I realized that my father had, in essence, killed my mother, or at least who she once was. Now she was my abuser's 2.0, an equivalent to the repulsive monster that had tortured me for the majority of my life.

It was all way too much, so I got in my fancy car and drove, sobbing continuously until I figured out how to process it.

And the award for worst Christmas in history goes to....

Even after all these years and all this journaling, I find that I am still upset, still angry, still resentful. It's not that I am offended that no one believed me. With the help of several therapists, I've become too secure for that. Rather, part of me is still in sheer shock. Everyone claimed to know me so well and after having known me for so many years, yet they never hesitated to assume that I was the one with the illness. They believed Father's lies, instantly and without any questions or hesitations.

Confusion. That's what all these memories bring. I don't even know how to comprehend several factors: A) I was in a situation where no one believed me despite the fact that they should've known my character. B) That one single person had absolutely no remorse for hurting the very people he claimed to love, especially his family. C) That everyone who claimed to have known me and cared so deeply for me so easily chose the side of the people who raised me and cast me aside like I was garbage. It was as if I were nothing at all.

My struggle for independence and healing culminated in a desperate—yet ultimately successful—bid for freedom, legally, emotionally, mentally, and financially, from my abusive father and equally abusive mother. After years of emotional manipulation, gaslighting, and attempts to isolate me, I finally secured a legal name change and a sealed court order to ensure my protection, effectively severing ties with my narcissistic father, ill mother, and his pervasive influence on all their friends and family. This hard-won autonomy, though not without lingering emotional scars and the tragic loss of Mother to Father's psychological manipulation, marked a pivotal turning point, allowing me to begin a new life free from his abuse and control.

The Letters

One of the counselors I had seen had instructed me to write letters to the people who hurt me and then burn them. While I like the idea, it just seems too risky. Apparently, even if someone has done you significant emotional harm, it's still illegal to light them on fire. So instead, I figured it would probably be a better idea just to write the letters.

To Mother,

Coincidentally enough, I happen to be writing this on your birthday. Although I've tried to forget the date many times, I can't seem to, no matter how many years have gone by. Despite the fact that you hurt me immensely, I hope this letter finds you well. I realize that you're quite sick mentally.

I hope you have finally figured out that Father's lies about how I don't care about you are untrue. I am still quite mad and equally disappointed that you allowed me to go through all of that and that you never stood up for me. But what can I even say? You left me no choice. I told you I had to leave in order to become healthy. I told you he was keeping me sick. And I told you these things over and over, day after day, for years.

You said you'd always be there for me, and that you needed me, but if that were true, you would be here with me now, celebrating your birthday and honoring the great and amazing person you used to be. But instead, I'm here without you, and you're no doubt dwelling on the fact that I am nowhere in sight, believing your husband's lies. I can just hear him now, grouping you in with him, saying, "We just weren't cut out to be parents." Instead of celebrating you, I try to forget you, because it's easier and less painful that way, especially knowing how deeply you hurt me, and that you continued to do so for several years on end. What's worse is that you never realized any of the deep hurt you caused, despite my repeatedly telling you so.

Even worse still is knowing that you aren't even close to who you used to be anymore. You're a shell of who you once were. Only the physical part of who you once were exists now. You're his 2.0, his perfect version of what he wanted you to become, torn down by insults that resulted in self-loathing. Now, you can't think on your own and only know to believe the things he has taught you to think.

I don't say this to hurt you, but I hope you realize that I wasted twelve extra, very long and agonizing years of my life, refusing to move out, just to try and save you from the monster he is, from the monster you've since become nearly equal to. I sacrificed my physical and mental health to continue living in that hell hole with that monster because I believed that you would one day realize the truth. I refused to leave you alone with him because I knew he would hurt you more if I wasn't around. Even after repeatedly telling you this, you still chose to stay with him. How do you think that felt knowing that my own mother would rather stay in a relationship with an abusive man than preserve her relationship with her own daughter who treated her well? How do you think it felt watching you cry after he insulted and berated you? How do you think it felt when my spending time with you didn't make you better? It made me feel like I was worthless. It made me feel completely unworthy. Unworthy of you, your love, or anything else for that matter.

I loved you very deeply and all I wanted, and desperately needed, was for you to love me back in the same way. But deep down I knew that you didn't, because if you did, you would've left him in order to help me. It took too long for me to realize this. I know now that you could never be capable of loving anyone, because you never learned to love yourself.

I loved you so incredibly deeply. You were my everything; my happiness, my hero, my confidant, my best friend. But that version of you no longer exists. You're not you anymore. After so many years of exposure to that toxicity, you've now become the 2.0 of the man who took the first thirty years of my life, the person who made me believe that I was nothing, the monster who made me believe that I wasn't even worthy of God's love.

That's why I had to leave that relationship. Because staying around that toxicity, those frequent insults, that constant negativity was poisoning me slowly. It was polluting me. It made me so sick that suicide was the only foreseeable option. But instead of realizing this was the cause of it, I was ridiculed for considering committing the "ultimate sin." I was deemed ungrateful and unlovable. I was avoided and cast aside. I became the one everyone loved to hate.

You could've prevented it and I even told you so countless times. Yet you chose to believe his lies. Then again, so did the majority of everyone else who ever met him...

What did you want me to do? Staying in that situation, even being around him for very little time, was way too much to handle. You wanted me to stay in that relationship and despite how many times I made it clear that doing so would keep me sick, you never cared or even heard me. My words went in one ear and out the other, as he so often claimed would occur with me.

What is it like to be with someone who treats you like shit? What's it like to allow your daughter to stay in such pain that she tried to end her life? What's it like to make excuses for a monster? Are these words bringing anything to light for you? Will you ever realize what horrible things you have allowed to happen? Or are you even capable of realization anymore?

And don't go blaming me like you did before. I made it perfectly clear that he made me sick, that I would never be capable of any quality of life if he was still around. I told you ample times that I would leave if he was still in the picture, and that I would never come back. I told you that you had lost my respect for allowing him to hurt us. It is not my fault that you chose to believe his lies that I was exaggerating and that that would never really happen. That is not my cross to bear, and now, after way too many years, I realize this. I did everything I could and then some, sacrificed way too much, more than anyone else would've. I am sorry you're unhappy, but I warned you that this would happen, and even offered you several outs that you didn't take. Looking back now, I think you were already too sick to even see the outs I was offering. I eventually realized that I can't save you if you don't want to be saved.

So now this is our reality. I'm here living my life, making a difference, and you're stuck in misery, left all alone to rot.

Why couldn't you see that I was trying desperately to help you avoid this?

Now, let's look back at your text, shall we?

"Well here we are a week later and I STILL can't believe my eyes."

Why can't you believe your eyes? I told you for years that I would leave and never come back unless he was out of the picture! Why can't you remember my telling you this, and that he is a monster, and about all the painful memories I recounted over and over, literally praying that you'd finally remember?

"Are you sure this is what you want?"

Hell, no, woman! This is definitely NOT what I want! How can you even ask that? You act like I have a choice, but if I'm to be healthy, I don't.

This is my worst nightmare turned into a reality, my worst fear come true, my most important prayer forever unanswered, and my heart and soul shattered into ten billion pieces, as every piece of me cries out for my Mommy, my savior from childhood, my best friend. Now the only thing left for me to do is to accept your decision to remain sick, and do the best I can to move on, without you, knowing that you're getting hurt, yet knowing you won't let anyone help you.

"Congratulations on your new home, an answer to many prayers on your behalf."

At least *your* prayers were answered. I can't say the same for my constant prayers over you.

"I guess all that's left to say is, Merry Christmas. My heart is broken."

Do you really think that I had a "Merry Christmas" spending my favorite holiday motherless, trying to process the fact that my own mother would rather stay with her abuser than be with me? How am I supposed to feel about that? If I had abused you too, then would you have considered staying with me?

I'm glad your heart just now broke. You've been breaking mine for over thirty years and never even noticed. You never felt it or heard it breaking, even though it was happening continuously, over and over, right in front of your eyes. Even after repeatedly telling you, you never once realized it.

So what now? It's hard for me. You were everything to me. And although I once thought I was everything to you too, I now know that that's not true. I used to think I wasn't enough for you. Now I realize that it was because you were never enough for yourself.

After you texted me that day, I got in my nice car, drove down the road like a bat out of hell, and sobbed continuously, mourning your loss. I know that physically you're alive, but he killed who you used to be. I still can't believe you let him and that you let him separate us. It was the most difficult day of my life. It would be easier if you were dead, then I would have the peace of mind of knowing he isn't hurting you, resting assured that you were in a better place. But this, I don't even know what to do with all of this.

Well, you'll be happy to know I'm now doing well. Or maybe you won't, as much as you act like your husband, I don't know anymore. While I hold your memory dearly in my heart, I have realized that it isn't safe for me to be around you, as much as it pains me to admit such things. Being without a mother left such a void in my heart, you know I always felt like I didn't belong anywhere. Losing you to an abusive asshole made that feeling even stronger, I hope you know.

Well guess what? I finally found somewhere I belong. This will upset you a great deal, but I found a new family. This family never makes me feel worthless or unwanted. I have gotten so much love and acceptance from this new family. As a matter of fact, I have two families, one who calls me their daughter, and another who calls me their "adopted daughter." Imagine that! All those years of feeling unworthy and I am now so desired and loved that I have two!

And, you're not going to believe this, but I have another kid now. Never wanting any kids, both were unexpected, but this one wasn't planned. The birth was rough but everything is okay now. We have a healthy baby boy. He looks so much like me, Mom. He's so happy and so full of life, and really enjoys all of his family and friends. He's perfect, just like my other son.

...But to be honest, it kills me knowing that you can't be here for any of this and that I can't share any of this with you. None of it. I realize that you died, Mom. You died years ago. Not that I would ever send this letter, but even if I did, the old you would never read it. It would be read by your husband's 2.0...

The old you would've been laughing with me if you'd been here right now. I've been crying as I write this and just blew my nose. You know how loud my nose blows are. Well, it woke the baby up from his nap and he let out a huge, full throttled scream...

Along with growing healthy, one also gains maturity. And through this maturity I have learned the real meaning of forgiveness. I used to think forgiveness was a way of letting slide the wrongdoings of people who committed harmful actions against us. However, I have since learned that forgiving someone does not at all mean that I have to allow that person back into my life, or that I ever have to tell a person that I forgive them, and that forgiving someone does not allow them any dominion over any aspect of my life. Rather, true forgiveness is a way of letting go of the hurts, unhealthy habits, and problems that a particular individual caused so that those aspects no longer have any bearing on one's life.

That being said, Mom, I forgive you for never remembering any of the memories that hurt me so deeply and negatively shaped my future. I forgive you for always prioritizing Father, as well as others in your life, over me. I forgive you for getting mad at me and being disappointed in me even when I did nothing to deserve such disappointment. I forgive you for saying that you couldn't sit with me even when I was about to end my life. I forgive you for always telling Father every secret I shared so deeply with you. I forgive you for never fully loving me and for never taking care of me the way you should have as my mother. I forgive you for allowing Father to hurt me. I forgive you because I don't want to keep holding onto the hurts and anger you caused by allowing the abuse. Those negative emotions do nothing for me, but rather act against me, keeping me perpetuating the same hurts, negative tendencies, and fear that caused me to have so many problems for so many long agonizing years.

I really do hope that one day you realize what I told you in that last text, "I love you, and hope that one day you realize that you don't deserve to be abused." And although we can't be together again in this life, I really hope that there is healing for you, and that we can meet again in the next life. Until then, Mom, beloved friend and idol, I will forever hold the memories we shared in a special place in my heart. I hope that the publication of this book helps create a legacy for you, as I believe you to be a martyr for others who are headed down the same path. And I pray that you find peace soon. And that this book helps any other person who is in a difficult relationship to find their self-worth so that they don't suffer a similar fate.

To Father,

How dare you still refer to yourself as my father. We both know, as per the information I had relayed to mother, that the relationship between us was dissolved in court. Therefore, you have no right to continue to refer to yourself as my father, and by far absolutely no right to refer to me as your daughter. Furthermore, I made it perfectly clear during a phone call that "Thanks to you, I spent the first thirty years of my life feeling sorry for everyone who had the burden of having me in their life. But now, *no* thanks to *you*, I finally realized that someone having me in their life is a privilege, not a burden. And a privilege you will no longer have because you refused to stop trying to rule over me."

You'll be disappointed to know that your snide response of, "You're *gonna* do what I say!" was not intimidating in the least.

What's it like to gain joy from ruling over another human being like they have no value? And what's it like to not even care? And why do you stay with your wife when you're clearly not happy? We both know you'd rather be completely alone with no one to make you feel bothered.

Or maybe being alone scares you. Maybe you felt alone when your father walked out on your mother, brother, and yourself. I know now that that made you feel rejected and undesirable, and made you feel like you were much less than what you wanted to be. And I realize now after all these years that you took it personally and still do to this day. Your mother never really talked about it so you just stuffed all those feelings down and internalized them. You kept the hurt inside, and it ate away at you. You knew you couldn't control your father leaving, so you became obsessed with what you could control. The hurt turned into anger and resentment and you became a narcissist so you wouldn't get hurt again. A narcissist who doesn't care what he does to others. And it got to the point that you even seemed to gain pleasure from controlling others, even when it hurts them. That, I will never understand.

I know your father hurt you but do you even realize how you hurt me? And how severely you did so? That you left me with gaping wounds that would take several years to heal? I think on some level you did know that but I think you wanted me to stay dysfunctional because you believe that everyone will leave you. You believe you're not worthy.

You're not worthy but you could've been. You chose to be a really mean person. Mean to the point that you gain joy from tearing others down. It sickens me.

It's disgusting how fake you are. How can you stand to display such fake caring around everyone who you claim is a friend or family member and then behind their backs talk shit about every one of them?

How can you stand to tear your wife down to the point that she's miserable and can't even stand to look at herself in the mirror because she hates who she sees staring back at her?

What's it like to always display a facade to be liked? What's it like to constantly spread lies about the person whom you claim is your daughter to the point that her entire support system turns away and abandons her? And in addition to that, you tore her down until she became so miserable that ending her life was the only foreseeable option for her.

Why? What's the point? Was existing in misery and self-loathing too much for you to bear alone that you decided to drag everyone around you down with you? If you're not happy, no one else can be, is that it?

I guess that's the one mutual thing we have to say about each other: I'll never understand you.

I'm not even going to try calling you out on all of the wrongs you committed against me, all of the insults you so carelessly aimed at me, or try to guilt trip you for making me so miserable. What's the point? You clearly don't even care that you're the meanest, most hateful, repulsive, repugnant individual I've ever had the displeasure of meeting. All you ever cared about was what was good for you, and what *you* wanted. It never mattered how anyone else felt as long as *you* were satisfied.

I spent many years hating your guts, wishing you dead, and contemplating doing bodily harm against you. Your constant insults, berating's, and slaps led me to hate you with every fiber of my being. It led me to despise you to the point that I used to fantasize how wonderful it would be if someone came to our door and notified Mother of your sudden, unexpected death. The truth is that deep down, your cruel words and hurtful actions led me to hate myself more than I hated anyone. So much so that eventually, I believed that even God didn't want me. For me to be so brutally honest with you when I confronted you via text about the harm you were causing me wasn't easy. I was always so terrified of you. And for you to have your friend call me trying to get information from me after I specifically asked for space was mind-blowing. You intentionally told her about that so that she would contact me knowing that she would report back to you. You knew that if I confided in her, she would break my trust and share it with you, and therefore you would have information to continually control me. You intentionally tried to make me stay mentally unwell so that no one else would want to keep me around.

You're a really sick person, and it took me so long to understand that that was why you treated me so badly. I used to think it was all my fault. But now I realize that it had nothing to do with me. I just really wish someone would've pointed all of this out to me during one of the myriad sessions of therapy, so that I could've learned this sooner. Then I wouldn't have wasted so much time hating myself, stuck in the cycle of the harmful behaviors I had observed from you and Mother.

Like I said, you're a really sick person. A person that doesn't care what he does to others as long as his own agenda is met. A person who takes pride in controlling others, no matter the cost. A person who doesn't care about lying to the ones he claims to love. A person with a fake personality around most people, who only shows his true personality to the people he lives with. A person who takes pride in hurting the person he claims is his daughter. A person who knows that his so-called daughter took legal action against him, yet still exploits this innocent woman any chance he gets. If people want to believe the lies that I am a horrible person who would just up and abandon my so-called family, so be it. I no longer care what others think. Anyone who knows me, really actually knows me, knows that I am the furthest thing from that kind of person.

You spent years telling me that I couldn't do anything, insinuating that I couldn't even take care of myself. From a young age, you constantly fed on my youthful insecurities with insults that tore me down. You tore down every dream I had, telling me that I would never get married, never be loved, never have a decent career, never have any nice things. You told me countless times when I was wanting to become a novelist that it was a pipe dream, that I wasn't talented enough. You said likewise about having a nice car. You spread countless lies about me in order to make yourself look good. You took my mom from me, making her believe the same shit you made me believe, that she isn't worth anything and is pathetic in every way. You did everything you could in an attempt to make sure that I would never and could never function properly without you.

You made me feel like the lowest of the low, for many long, agonizing years. You ultimately led me to believe that I wasn't even worthy of God's love. One day I realized that you are just a scared little child who never grew up, because you never worked to overcome your own insecurities. When I realized this, everything changed for me.

Guess what, old man? You were wrong. Dead wrong. About all those things. I am loveable. I am worthy. I am enough. The fact that I am not enough for you has nothing to do with me, and everything to do with you and your own insecurities and the illnesses caused by the things you never addressed about your own hurts.

I may not have Mom anymore, I can't help that. I've learned to aim for the sky, despite all of your negativity. I bought my fancy car without your help. I am happily married to an amazing man who treats me right and honestly values me above all else. We are on our way to owning our house, something else you always said would never happen for me. We have two amazing kids who are perfect. I worked my way through school while working two part time jobs. I have a great job that I love, working at the company I founded all by myself, a company that works to fight the stigma and the problems that people like you so hatefully create. I became a contributing writer in my fields of expertise. I have amazing parents and other extended family who love me deeply and make me feel valued. These are people I actually enjoy spending time with, and who don't feel like a job I'm not paid enough to spend time with. I have a myriad of amazing friends who also love me and who have continually been there for my family and I in a lot of amazing ways. And now, I am the author of a published book. It's not a novel, but a book I never intended to publish. Ironically, it contains the journals I wrote as a part of therapy for the immense pain and severe problems you caused me.

In other words, I have learned to take the high road and use the pain and suffering I lived through to help others. And now, because of that mindset shift, I have everything you told me I never would, and then some.

...As well as the last laugh, albeit unintentionally.

Has constantly guarding yourself from others been worth all that effort in the end? You must realize that the court case I filed against you, as well as the fact that I'm now running my own company working in mental health, makes me look quite credible. That poses a threat to all your continued lies, evident by the fact that the Robbins family, whom about a year ago were willing to refer people to me, suddenly are avoiding me and now believe that my name never changed (evident by a phone call I made to Mrs. Robbins the other day). I sensed that they were pulling away from me again, and now that Mrs. Robbins never called me back as she said she would, plus her daughter clearly avoiding me, makes me realize that you have been intentionally dragging my name through the mud, as usual. Not that I expect you'll ever stop. As healthy as I am, and with all my qualifications, I wonder what exactly you said or did to make them question me and pull away from me again. It's unfortunate for them. I had been calling to obtain their permission to have their son's name memorialized in print within the dedication of this book. But now they will never have that honor, nor will he.

It's sad really, that you feel the need to continue discrediting me after all these years. You turned my entire should've-been support system away from me, wasn't that enough? And now, in addition to the trauma you've caused in my life, how many people who need help haven't contacted me because you have been telling all of the people you know not to use my services? I'm sure you've also made it a point to tell them to let everyone they know not to use my company. Did anyone die by suicide or a drug overdose who would've contacted me, but didn't, because you are so convincing when you claim that I am the one who is mentally unstable and that I am also supposedly autistic? What's it like to not care who you hurt, or who gets hurt due to your need for people's constant attention and admiration?

Well, go ahead. Slander away. Drag my name through the mud, intentionally, and with every chance you get. I have enough people in my life now who are genuine and realize the truth. They realize that I, as well as my colleagues, are all really great at what we do. They all know that my company is a legitimate one that provides reputable, very valuable services that cannot be obtained elsewhere. Our clients know this as well. So do our associates. I am even verified through the Medical Fitness Network, so that alone indicates that my name and business are legitimate. Eventually, all of your lies will snowball into an avalanche you can't keep up with...and you'll be caught. Eventually, people will realize that you're the one with an illness, not me. You know this, which is why you continue to work so hard to discredit me, to make people focus on my supposed illness so they won't recognize yours. Eventually, people will realize all of this. When they do, just remember what you told me: the truth will set you free.

Here's a question to ask yourself honestly: What do you even really have in life? And I'm not talking about things like your house or car or fancy vacations. Those are just things. Things don't matter in the end when all is said and done. You can't even say that you have people who love you, because they love the person you're pretending to be. Have you considered that at your funeral, those people won't really be mourning or missing *you*?

They'll miss the facade of the man you're pretending to be. If people found out what you're really like, who would actually, truly miss you?

Seriously. What do you honestly have, other than negativity and misery? Why anyone would choose to lead such a life is beyond me.

Despite all the horror you put me through, I have learned to forgive you. I forgive you for hurting myself and my mother. I forgive you for making me hate myself, and for making me hate Mother. I forgive you for all the lies you told to discredit me. I even forgive you knowing that you will continue to do so, and always will. You will undoubtedly convince everyone you know that this entire narrative is nothing more than a huge delusion that exists only in my head, and I forgive you for that, too. I forgive you for intentionally turning everyone against me, for making my entire support system except for one friend abandon me when I needed help most and for the isolation you deliberately caused me. I forgive you for the problems you caused me that once ruled my life because of everything you did. I forgive you for making me believe I was incapable of doing anything. I forgive you for all the hard work you caused me to have to do in therapy to process and heal from all of that. I forgive you for stealing Mother away from me. I forgive you for everything you stole from me: my friends, my family, my neighbors, my deceased friends' parents, the referral network I could have leveraged as a business owner, my happiness, my confidence, my sanity, my security, my sense of self-worth, my positivity, my Mother, and even for the many years you stole from my life that I can never get back. I am proud to admit to you, and to myself, that I have grown to the point that I will no longer allow you or anyone else, including myself, to steal more time from my valuable life. I no longer succumb to the fear or nervousness that your lies used to instill in me. Enough people know me now, really truly know me, who realize what's actually true and what's not. Enough people do believe me. Now that you're out of my life, I have been able to be healthy, in every sense of the word. I have more people in my corner now than I ever did before, and much more strength as well. Life is way too short to regret one's mistakes, especially when they were the result of malicious actions carried out by someone other than oneself.

A New Life

All of the torment, the confusion, the agony, the wasted efforts to tell the truth, the wasted attempts and many wasted years trying to get Mother to see the truth was all way too much. And in the end, all I could do was keep asking the universe, myself, and the Heavens, "what was it all for?"

Father took so much from me: my dignity, my physical health, my mental health, love for myself and others, confidence in myself, faith in humanity, time that I cannot get back, efforts that were wasted, faith in a higher power, my will to live, and ultimately, my mother. He made it so I had almost nothing left. I had nothing left to lose, nothing to be thankful for, and ultimately not one single thing left to live for.

Afterwards, I continued to hate him for it, as I had for so many years. What else could be expected when hatred and evil were all that I was taught? But now I also hated my mother for allowing all of that to happen to me as well as to herself. That was a feeling I had never experienced towards her until then.

I honestly don't know why I kept going, why I even continued to the next day. With all those odds against me, it really doesn't make sense, does it? Maybe it was fear of death that kept me here on this earth, or the fear of almost succeeding at suicide but instead becoming incapacitated. Maybe it was the deep seeded desire to be truly loved, instead of merely being told that I was loved by people who never learned to love themselves. Or maybe it was the searing desire to feel like I was of value to any other human being other than myself. Whatever the reason, I can honestly say that I'm glad I did keep fighting. I know this must sound absolutely insane after everything in the previous chapters, but much good actually came out of several of the negative events that transpired. After all that agony and torment, I finally waged many victories.

The intense isolation made me realize that I had to take care of myself because no one else really would. This realization provided me with the emotional resilience and mental strength I needed to learn how to fend for myself. Now I possess strength during times of adversity, as well as a strong sense of independence and self-reliance. This equipped me with the perfect training, in addition to my schooling, to ensure that, as a mental health practitioner, I remain professional and look at everything without my own personal bias.

The struggle had ingrained in me a severe determination and strong willpower, which helped me to show up for myself at the gym every day, three hours a day, for the last eight and a half years. I lost sixty-six pounds within two years, and have gone from shirt size 3X to XS, with muscles to show for all my hard work.

Through the assaults, I gained determination never to be a victim again, a reason to finally leave my house on a regular basis, and the motivation I needed to devote enough time and work hard enough to gain the physical strength I now possess. Weight lifting has become a favorite hobby of mine, even though I hate exercising. I realize that doesn't make a whole lot of sense to most people, but for me, knowing I am strong enough to lift more than I weigh gives me much satisfaction, and obviously, confidence as well. Even still, I continue to show up at the gym daily, making sure that I grow even stronger. I am also now a certified kickboxing instructor, so I also possess a lovely set of self-defense skills and strategies.

One of the friends who turned their back on me also subsequently turned her back on her so-called "best friend" and abandoned her when her health took a turn for the worse. The "best friend" that that person abandoned has now become my second best friend, and one of two amazing godmothers to my youngest son.

After I was acquitted from therapy, so to speak, I reached back out to my former therapist to thank her and check in on her, and we've since become good friends as well as business associates. As a matter of fact, she is now a member of my team. She has played a pivotal role in my company by helping me to gain the knowledge I need as well as advocating for the need for the specific services that I provide.

Despite all statistical odds, I managed to break the addictions of all of the prescription medications that I had been prescribed and have learned ways to better cope rather than taking the harmful chemicals. Contrary to what the psychiatrist had told me, I discovered that I won't really "always need to be on some kind of medication in order to function properly." After several horrifying experiences of my own as well as talking with others who shared their own medication horror stories, I became educated about the real risks of being prescribed mediation that are often not outrightly shared with patients. Now a big part of what I do with my company is to educate people on the hidden risks of prescription drugs and help them navigate the many unfortunate side effects they cause, as well as the addictions.

The judgment and hatred I endured at the hands of so many created a unique gift in me. I now possess a specific and rare skill set of empathy and discernment that allows me to provide mental health care to those in need. I am told by clients that I am an expert at viewing things from their point of view and at anticipating their needs. I have also been told that I possess a unique gift that cannot be learned or taught, and that even therapists don't possess the abilities that I do.

Because of all of those things, I was able to pursue an education to accompany my skillset, working two to four part time jobs at a time while putting myself through school. It was far from easy, and the schedule was really too much, but eventually, I completed my schooling. After several failed attempts at seeking steady employment within the fitness or mental health industries, I grew tired of the two year long struggle, and also realized that the type of company I was looking to work for did not yet exist. So, after much consideration, debate, and a serious conversation with my healthy parents that I have now, I decided to launch my own company. One that specializes in mental health, suicidal ideation, and the aftercare that stress centers, rehab facilities, and therapy alone do not adequately provide to those struggling with a mental health crisis, addiction, or both. My company works closely in conjunction with other physical and mental health professionals to provide a complete umbrella of comprehensive care that is lacking within the mental health industry.

In addition to running my own company, I also provide motivational speeches. I really enjoy helping others transform their trauma into triumph. Through my speeches, I teach others that they don't have to remain a slave to the trauma they endured and that it is up to each individual to choose their own destiny.

In hindsight, if I had succeeded in my suicide attempts, none of this would be a reality now. My company would not exist, so then there would still be no adequate aftercare for mental health. The people I have helped would never have met me, so they may not have had the skillset to change their lives for the better. My oldest son would not have any kind of healthy mother figure and would not have been promoted to big brother status, and my youngest son would never have come to be. And if a cause this great is my destiny, I wonder what theirs might be.

I am very grateful that I listened to that inner voice deep inside of me that told me that I *was* being treated badly, despite the fact that no one around me wanted to believe it. I pressed onward, and eventually gained the courage and strength to stand up and fight for myself even though no one else would until several long years later. Although I really don't know exactly what I was doing or how to fight the battles that I did, I simply tried for the life I finally figured out that I deserved. It wasn't easy, and was a messy, long, hard, exhausting road, but I did it. I ignored the frustrations, the injustices, the anxieties, the anger, and endured the hatred and hurts of those who chose to think less of me. I put myself out there, awkwardly and uncomfortably, until I had learned to face the social fears caused by so many who refused to believe me, or who discarded me like an insignificant piece of trash. I sought help to overcome the habits caused by those hurts and spent many long, painful years of working to rectify my shortcomings and faults, so that eventually I could create a better life for myself. I accomplished my goal of living, actually living, rather than stalely existing. And now I'm helping to ignite that same courage, inner strength, and warrior spirit in others who need to find it within themselves. I am so honored to be able to help others in such a pivotal way and enjoy watching others make the ascension out of the ashes of the hell they once knew.

The couple who went out of their way to stand up for me and help me when no one else would have since become my parents as well as the legal next of kin for my youngest son, in the event of a tragedy. While it is quite sad knowing that the mother that raised me is extremely sick and thus incapable of recovering at this point, it helps knowing that I finally have people who really do care and love me the way parents are supposed to. Because of them, my youngest son has grandparents, great grandparents, aunts, uncles, and cousins who care for him as well as lift him up in positivity rather than tearing him down. I know he will grow up healthy, happy, and will not live with the same hurts, dysfunctions, and roadblocks that his older brother and I were forced to.

After years of working through all the pain, rage, and hatred that I once had, as well as many sessions of therapy, I eventually learned to forgive the parents that hurt me. It was actually rather easy once I learned that they had held onto a myriad of hurts and dysfunctions of their own that they never addressed or even acknowledged. Upon learning about each of those, I realized that I was a much bigger person. I was more mature than they were. I finally realized that, because I was working steadily to address my hurts and dysfunctions in therapy, I always would be.

Mark Twain was quoted as saying, "Anger is an acid that does more harm to the vessel in which it is stored than to anything onto which it is poured." In other words, possessing anger doesn't do much to the person one is angry with and really only hurts the angry person in the long run.

My husband once pointed out to me that the old saying is true: "The best revenge is living well." I later thought about it another way, realizing how glad Paul would be if I was still upset and dysfunctional. He would have the pride of thinking that I couldn't function without him. On the other hand, I don't think Paul would be happy at all knowing that I am doing much better than most people since I removed him from my life. Based on the success I'm living, I'd say that the saying is one hundred percent accurate. Look back at the letter I wrote to him. I'm sure he can't be living too well after all the negative energy he's spent years putting into the world, albeit covertly. I strongly believe that what goes around comes around and that people eventually get back the negativity, or positivity, they think or feel.

I hope that this story helps others to process their trauma and regulate emotions, as well as aiding in letting go of the anger caused by the hurt and injustices they have suffered. It took me too many long agonizing years to realize that one really does have control of their own destiny by being taught how to regulate the way they react to things. Although we have no control over the world or the others in it, we do control how we react to our trauma. It doesn't have to define us, or who we will become, or how we can or should live our life. Our experiences don't have to break us, paralyze us, or cause us to live in fear. We choose how we react to things. We decide whether to put in the work to make the changes necessary to improve ourselves so that we can eventually live our best life, or whether we will remain a slave to our trauma, allowing it to continue to alter our life.

Life is never easy. It's full of ups and downs, struggles and strengths, adversity and trauma, hope and resilience. I know what you're thinking, and you're right. Life is far from fair. People have unfair advantages in life that you will never have, making things naturally easier for them than it will ever be for you. It's not fair, it's not right, and it just sucks, I get it. But it is up to each individual to decide how they will react to their unfair circumstances. In other words, *you* decide how to react after trauma. *You* decide to thrive afterward, or to shut down and live in fear. *You* decide whether to put in the long, hard, difficult work or simply to not try, thus embracing misery. People should ask themselves: Do I want to be the one who succumbed into nothingness, or the one who rose up above despite what happened to me? The one who succumbed to the unfair circumstances or the one who makes the best out of the worst? Do I want the people who caused the problems to have the pleasure of knowing that the problems are continuing without them, making them feel that I cannot succeed if they're not in my life? Or do I want to live a great life despite them abandoning me, forcing them to realize that I really am better off without them?

Even if everything is working against you, keep going, and try your hardest. Even if you have no family and no friends, find a reason to go on. Find a reason to survive and then prove all the haters wrong by thriving instead of merely surviving. Make them jealous at your resilience in the face of adversity. Turn the injustices, hatred, anger, and jealousy into a positive by using them to motivate you. Make it work for you instead of against you.

After all that I have been through, I am proud that I can now say I take pride in the struggle, I have learned to smile through adversity, and I laugh in the face of fear and uncertainty. I embrace every day for what it is: potentially the last day I have on this earth. Tomorrow is never a guarantee. I am proud to say that I have, after many long, painful, agonizing, lonely years, learned to embrace every day as a gift.

Again, I know it's not easy, and that at times life sucks, but I hope this book inspires anyone that needs it to rise above. I hope that this book ignites a fire within others to stand up for what's right, to be the change they wish to see within the world. I hope that, if you're struggling with life, or struggling just to make it through one more agonizing day, that my story of trauma and recovery, despite all odds, ignites a fire within you that maybe you didn't even know you had. If all odds are against you, I hope you keep fighting. I hope you decide to shoot for the stars. I know working on oneself is a lot of work and that it's definitely far from fun, but it's worth it in the end.

Above all else, never forget this: despite what anyone else may tell you, you *are* enough. And know that even if no one else does, I believe in you.

Although I no longer participate in organized religion, I have become quite spiritual. Yes, I have a relationship with a higher power again and it's better than it ever was before. Through my relationship with God, I let go of the hurts, insecurities, and pain from my trauma. I've learned to forgive my former mother, and, miraculously, even my former father. Through a small group of open, like-minded individuals, however, I eventually realized that I still blamed myself for staying in that situation for so long and for allowing each of the unsafe situations to happen. I realized that I hated myself for allowing the parental abuse to go on for so long. I realized that, despite all other aspects of healing, I still hated myself for not realizing earlier how far gone Mother truly was.

One night, I admitted to the members of that small group that I had yet to forgive myself. I sort of had, but hadn't fully done so. I hadn't acknowledged the feelings I had experienced as well as some of the things I had done because I had felt that I should do them or that I didn't have a choice in the matter.

Unlike any small group that I had participated in before, these people had also shared their deepest, dirtiest secrets within our little sacred space. Each one of them felt more than warm and accepting, they felt equal to me rather than the typical "holier than thou", (you know the type), I have felt before. They felt safe and, quite honestly, they felt like home.

This would explain why, within that small group, that sacred space, I shared a deeply personal letter I had written. It was the letter of amends I had written to myself. For the first time ever, I shared freely and uninhibitedly. With absolutely no reservations or hesitations, I read the letter aloud to the small group of newfound friends. This was vastly different than anytime I had shared things before. I felt a sense of calm and acceptance wash over me as I read my letter, containing all the things I had been holding onto that I was still ashamed of. As I read, the waterworks started, and I began sobbing uncontrollably. Despite my raw, vulnerable emotional state, I still felt comfortable...and what's more, I still felt one-hundred percent accepted. That feeling of acceptance was new to me, but my ability to share openly, to really, honestly and uninhibitedly, was even more new to me. Never before had I ever been able to cry in front of anyone other than my former parents. I had never even cried in front of therapists or even my best friend of several years. That's when I realized that I had always been subconsciously terrified of being vulnerable, even in front of seemingly safe spaces. It made sense, given my lengthy history of repeated abandonment.

As I continued to read the letter, as well as continuing to sob profusely, I didn't sense anyone feeling uncomfortable or judgy, rather I sensed eyes gazing upon me with genuine concern and appreciation for sharing such intimate personal details about my heaviest guilt in life.

When I finished reading the letter, it literally felt as if a weight had been lifted off of me. It almost felt as if each member of this small group had taken on a chunk of the stone that had been crushing me, making it much lighter than it had been before. This was when I realized that, within this sacred space, this amazing small group, I was never alone, and never would be again. And with that realization, my sobbing stopped, and a feeling of warmth emanated throughout my heart. I took a deep breath as the feeling slowly pulsed throughout the rest of my body. This, I learned that night, was Celebrate Recovery.

So, without further adieu, here it is: the final piece of this crazy puzzle, the end of this chapter of my unbelievable life situation, the letter of amends I wrote to myself years ago, forgiving the old, weak, insecure, terrified me for the crimes committed against the new, much better, stronger, resilient me. This was when I let go and gained my real freedom.

Dear Self....

Dear self,

For all the praise I publicly gave him on Facebook because it was too hard to handle the painful truth, I'm sorry.

For all the praise I gave him because I felt obligated since that's what he often told me, I'm sorry.

For believing every insult and put down he said to me was true, I'm sorry.

For allowing him to dictate what I should think, say, feel, do, wear, and listen to, I'm sorry.

For the many agonizing years I lived in fear of speaking the truth against him, I'm sorry.

For allowing him to convince me that his lies were the truth, I'm sorry.

For the many traumatic memories that fear caused me to suppress for so long, I'm sorry.

For believing that I deserved every harsh ridicule and painful slap, I'm sorry.

For living with paralyzing fear and shame for countless years and not realizing that I COULD and SHOULD establish boundaries, I'm sorry.

For buying into his lies that you are autistic and unable to function in any setting without "freaking out," I'm sorry.

For believing everyone else who refused to believe you because they bought into his pretty lie instead of the ugly truth, I'm sorry.

For all the times I sold out and pretended to be who someone else wanted me to be just so I could try to gain a friend, I'm sorry.

For every slice, scratch, bruise, and cigarette I inflicted upon you in an attempt to erase the pain, I'm sorry.

For every poor decision made in an attempt to have anyone else other than myself see your value, I'm sorry.

For all the times you cried out to God, broken and abandoned on the floor, believing you were unwanted even by the Lord Himself, I am really, truly, sorry.

I have continued to be sorry for several years, thinking back about the things I shouldn't have believed, the things I shouldn't have done because no one else could see the truth, and I have continued to hate you so deeply for it. I have hated you for all the years you stole from the me that I am now, for all the experiences you will never get to have now because the opportunity has long passed, for all the people you didn't get enough time with that have passed on, for all the long-term health problems that are side effects from all the chemicals in the pills that you so willingly took because your elders told you that you needed them. I have hated you for always being paralyzed by fear, for always perceiving yourself as weak and insignificant. And for all of these things, I am truly sorry as well.

You were a mere child at the time, thrown into a series of unexpected situations that were emotional, horrible, misleading, and confusing. You always hated yourself, but finally realized that you are me, the older, wiser, stronger version that you were always created to be. You didn't have anyone to help you cope or understand any of the things that were going on. You had no idea how to react or what to do about any of it. You were too young to fend for yourself adequately, so you tried your best. It wasn't good enough for you at the time, because it wasn't good enough for anyone else. But I am here now to tell you that it *was* good enough, you *were* good enough, YOU ARE ENOUGH! You made it this far, farther than all of the statistics say you should have. According to all the statistics, you should be an alcoholic, never have been able to stop taking the medicine, a drug addict, have liver, kidney, or blood disease, or all of the above. You shouldn't be able to hold down a steady job, and you should wind up dead, or at the very least, destitute, like most people who grew up in the sort of situations that you did. You fought your hardest, did your best, and took care of yourself, even though no one else would and despite the fact that no one else could see it. You survived, and best of all, you are thriving. And you finally know that YOU ARE WORTHY.

And with that, I finally learned to really, truly, fully love myself.

Helpful Tips and Resources

Helpful Tips for Establishing Boundaries: (Say these out loud to yourself when you're doubting yourself, when you know you're being gaslit, when you're ready to reclaim your power.)

It is not my responsibility to rescue others from their drama.

It is ok for me to tell people no.

I do not always have to explain myself.

It is ok if others get angry with me.

It is ok to take time to make myself happy and do the things that bring me joy.

I will distance myself from those who tell me how I should think, feel, or be.

It is ok if others don't agree with me.

It is ok if people don't like me, but it is not ok for someone to disrespect me or the boundaries I have established.

I do not need permission to do the things that make me happy.

I do not need permission to be who I am or feel what I feel.

I will not allow people to make me feel obligated to do things.

I have a right to stay away from those who want more from me instead of for me.

It is not ok if people think they have the right to abuse me, physically, verbally, or emotionally, which includes family, my partner, friends, and coworkers.

No one has the right to disrespect myself, my boundaries, or others I care about.

I have a right to choose to end toxic relationships with those who drain the energy out of me, including family, my partner, friends, and coworkers.

I am enough for myself and should not need anyone else, although that doesn't mean I don't want to spend time with those who bring me joy and happiness.

Copyright Crimson Holistic Wellness, 2022

Resources:

American Foundation for Suicide Prevention (AFSP)- https://afsp.org Be connected to resources for people who are at risk, connections to mental health resources, information for those who are having thoughts of suicide, resources for survivors of loss, connection to support groups, resources for surviving a loss and what to do afterward.

National Domestic Violence Hotline, Hours: 24/7, (800)799-7233. Text BEGIN to 88788. Multiple languages available.

The National Child Traumatic Stress Network (NCTSN)- https://n ctsn.orgResources about various types of child trauma, treatments and practices, information and care resources for various types of trauma. 988-Hotline. Hours 24/7. Call in the event of crisis, including suicidal ideation or substance use. Text TALK to 741741. Available in English or Spanish.

Substance Abuse and Mental Health Services Administration (SAMH-SA)- https://samhsa.govInformation and resources on substance use disorders as well as mental health resources.

Celebrate Recovery- https://celebraterecovery.comA Christ-centered group of people who work through their hurts, hang-ups, and habits in a close-knit, safe space.

Alcoholics Anonymous (AA)- https://aa.org

Narcotics Anonymous (NA)- https://na.org

About the Author

Putting herself through school while working 2 jobs with a mortgage and young family, Tambryn made a complete career change from assistant manager at a restaurant and embarked on her new journey in the fitness industry. Originating from a broken home and dissatisfied with the lack of comprehensive care within the mental health industry, she obtained more schooling within the psychology field, and eventually, Crimson Holistic Wellness was born. She is a certified Trauma Healing Practitioner, a certified Attachment Based Family Therapy Suicide Prevention advocate, an Addiction Recovery Specialist, Nutritionist, and Fitness Coach. She helps others achieve mental health by focusing specifically on depression, anxiety, attachment ruptures, and overall mental wellbeing by cultivating healthy relationships and reinforcing positive mindset and affirmations.

Tambryn started pursuing an education within the mental health industry after creating her own successful wellness journey. After surviving an abusive home where she was more than double her healthy recommended weight, a lethargic prediabetic with severe depression, crippling anxiety, with a prescription addiction, and self-harm issues, she eventually made the difficult but necessary decision to forever say goodbye her abusers and embark on a new life. Within 4 years, she was down to a shirt size XS and was proudly no longer relying on the need for prescription medications, unhealthy junk foods, self-harm, and cigarettes to get through the day.

She uses her expertise to design personalized programs that implement specific needs and desires of her clients, and focuses on helping individuals who have also endured verbal, psychological, mental, physical, and sexual abuse. She provides an active support system in which she utilizes her expertise and experience to help others achieve the happy, healthy life they deserve. Her favorite part of her job is knowing that not only is she creating a healthier, happier life for her clients, but they, in turn, are helping her create a stronger voice to end the stigma that still so strongly surrounds mental health and addiction.

Although having her own company is a huge undertaking, Tambryn is very active in the community, participating in local relationship groups, helping support food pantries and animal shelters, and working closely in conjunction with the non-profit organization American Foundation for Suicide Prevention.

When she is not working, her main focus is on her husband and two sons, and also her gigantic family of 2 loving parents, stellar grandparents, several siblings, and a multitude of nieces and nephews. She enjoys driving, axe-throwing, weight lifting, and boxing in her spare time (she is also a certified kickboxing instructor).

www.ingramcontent.com/pod-product-compliance
Lightning Source LLC
Chambersburg PA
CBHW070617130626
46556CB00001B/398